STORM
TOSSED

HOW A U.S. SERVICEMAN
WON THE BATTLE OF
SEX ADDICTION

STORM
TOSSED

How a U.S. Serviceman
Won the Battle of
Sex Addiction

Jake Porter

CLADACH
Publishing

Published by CLADACH Publishing
PO Box 336144 Greeley, CO 80633
www.cladach.com
© 2006 by John Buzzard
Published under the pseudonym *Jake Porter*

This is a personal memoir based on the author's experiences
and surrounding events as he remembers them. Many other individuals were involved in these events. Because of the sensitive
nature of many of the events and conversations recorded herein,
many names, physical descriptions, and circumstances have been
changed to protect the privacy of these individuals.

Printed in the USA

Scripture quotations, unless otherwise noted, are taken from the
Holy Bible, New International Version, NIV. Copyright 1973,
1978, 1984 by International Bible Society. Used by permission of
Zondervan Publishing House. All rights reserved.

Cover Photo © James W. Mitchell

Library of Congress Control Number: 2005935971

ISBN-13: 978-0-9759619-0-2
ISBN-10: 0-9759619-0-X

TABLE OF CONTENTS

FOREWORD

In Isaiah 61 the prophet gave a remarkable picture of the anointing that would be on the coming Messiah. He uses a phrase, "the year of the Lord's favor." We have been living in that "year" for close to 2,000 years now. Jesus quoted from this passage at the start of His ministry saying that He was the fulfillment of this scripture. I believe this same anointing that was on Jesus is to be on His people today.

Consider some of these phrases from the passage:

> The Spirit of the Sovereign LORD is on me, because the LORD has anointed me to preach good news to the poor. He has sent me to bind up the brokenhearted, to proclaim freedom for the captives and release from darkness for the prisoners, to proclaim the year of the LORD's favor. (Isaiah 61:1-2)

The further our society moves away from Christianity, the more we are finding people who are in need of the provisions mentioned in this scripture. As my wife Linda and I moved into the ministry mentioned here in Jake's story, we had no idea as to the immensity of the pain, shame, and guilt the average person is walking around with in our society here in North America. Most of the ones we pray for have been going to church for much of their lives and are still carrying burdens that were paid for at Calvary. The provision is there for all of us. The problem is not with the Redeemer. He has done His work. What are missing are the place and the time for us to off-load these weights.

I was on a flight a few years ago, and as I sat down the gentleman next to me volunteered that he was searching the great religions of the world for the answers to life. He was a university professor and had come to a crossroads in his life where he was honestly searching. He had been going to church and it seemed pointless.

"What do you do?" he asked.

Laughingly, I told him I had been in missions for the past twenty-five years.

"Give me your best shot," responded the inquirer.

"Okay. Here is your life," I said while holding my hands about eighteen inches apart. "Here is your birth and here is today. Back here, before today, is a messed up life—pain, sin, shame, and guilt. Right?"

"You said it!" he replied.

"What do you do with all this stuff?" I asked.

"That's why we're having this conversation," he said. "That's why reincarnation is looking really good to me right now."

"Right," I agreed. "If you only have one chance at life, you're in big trouble. That is one of the things that is so profound about our faith. We have a redeemer who paid the price for all of this—the sin, the pain, the shame, and the guilt. He takes the load off of us and places it on Himself. This is what the Cross is all about. Then He gives us a new life and we walk in freedom."

The man pondered this in silence for about thirty seconds. Then came his summation. "That's a hell of a deal!"

That man saw the truth of the Cross that day.

Jake Porter experienced this truth personally. I have known Jake since he was in the fifth grade with our own son. Consequently, it was all the more wonderful to be able to watch his transformation take place. Even though this is Jake's story, I have heard this story replayed thousands of times. Oh yes, each story differs a bit here and there. However, the result is always the same. The teller has ended up encumbered to the point of wondering if there is ever such a thing as freedom from his or her load.

We never tire of the experience of watching a person come into this marvelous freedom. We have witnessed it thousands of times in the last decade and with the release of each prisoner we rejoice as we did with the first people we prayed for. What a wonderful Redeemer! Thank You, Lord Jesus!

Jerry Praetzel, Montana
International Bible Teacher

1
RAT POISON

No one can serve two masters. Either he will hate the one and love the other, or he will be devoted to the one and despise the other. You cannot serve both God and money. Matthew 6:24

THE .357 MAGNUM pointed in my face looked more seductive than any woman I had ever been to bed with. Oh, how I wished for the tenacity to pull the trigger. Outside, it was another cold gray day with an inch of snow on the ground. I was alone in my room. Around me were mementos of shattered dreams and unfulfilled ambitions. What had happened? I was feeding my family with food stamps, the government was paying my rent, and I was on academic probation at the University of Montana.

Shooting myself seemed like an easy escape route, yet each time I tried to end my life something stopped me. An indescribable fear of the unknown would hit me as I approached the brink of death. Why the constant failures? And why did I, a Christian, desire to kill myself? What brought all this on? Where was God, anyway?

• • •

At the age of four, I had become angry, confused, and afraid of the dark. It was June 28, 1970—a warm and pleasant Sunday evening in Glendora, California. Night brought a welcome relief from the dry heat that had dominated the day. I was kneeling at the foot of my bed that was covered with the Snoopy bedspread, and I was playing with a plastic toy motorcycle when my mom entered the room. Riding on her left hip was my two-month old baby sister, Marie. My parents had adopted her the month before in Santa Rosa, California and I'd been just as excited as my grandparents when Mom and Dad had walked into the house with her. The baby now looked at me with her dark brown eyes.

"What's your brother doing?" Mom said while stroking Marie's thick black hair.

Mom turned to me. "Honey, get your pajamas packed. Grandma and Grandpa are taking you to the cabin tonight."

Grandma and Grandpa! The cabin! Nothing filled a four year old with more excitement than the expectation of being spoiled by his grandparents. I jumped to my feet and began filling my small, musty brown suitcase with PJs, underwear, and socks. Then I anxiously waited in the living room. My dad, dressed in his tan uniform, fastened his duty belt and prepared to spend another night on the freeways of Los Angeles working for the highway patrol.

At last my grandparents arrived, and we were off to their weekend home, known to the family as "The Cabin," in the San Bernardino Mountains. We arrived late, so Grandma fixed me a quick snack then tucked me into bed.

The next morning I sat at the breakfast table eating cornflakes and watching sun rays shine through the pine trees and listening to the squawking blue jays. Grandma was in the kitchen. Grandpa had gone to work.

Suddenly, the lady who lived in the house behind the cabin appeared in the sliding glass door I was looking through and began knocking. "Dorothy, Dorothy," she called.

Grandma opened the door. "Betty, what's the matter?"

"You've got an emergency phone call, come quick!"

"Jake, stay here and finish your cereal. I'll be right back!" Then Grandma and the neighbor scurried up the hill.

Nervously I sat there in my pajamas, chewing my corn flakes.

When Grandma returned, her face was pale and tears had formed behind her glasses. "Jake, get dressed right now. I have to take you home."

"Why?"

"Just do as I say."

During the drive back to Glendora, I kept asking Grandma what was the matter, but she never answered. When we arrived at our house it was filled with relatives wearing dress clothes. The ladies were crying and the men were grim. As I walked through the living room, everyone watched me. Everyone had white China cups of coffee sitting on saucers, but no one drank.

My mother led me into the kitchen and knelt down, I could tell she had been crying. Looking me in the face she plainly stated, "Jake, Marie isn't with us anymore."

Scared and confused I asked, "Where did she go?"

"Jesus took her to be with Him in Heaven." Years later she admitted she had used a poor choice of words.

Filled with rage, I blurted, "I hate Jesus for taking my sister!"

"No, no, sweetie, don't say that," she pleaded.

I didn't repeat it, but I meant it with all my heart.

That morning, when Mom had gotten out of bed to check on the baby, she had felt the presence of the Holy Spirit as if He was preparing her for something dreadful. In the crib, she found Marie lifeless and cold.

The funeral was held at the Nazarene church we attended, but I didn't go. They took me to the gravesite where her headstone was adorned with flowers and toy windmills. Nearby stood a statue of a grieving little boy holding a cowboy hat in one hand and a bouquet in the other. I stared at it. The statue would occasionally appear in my dreams throughout my life.

I was afraid that Jesus would kill me next. Since church was "God's House" I believed Jesus was lurking there and would punish us for trespassing. I couldn't understand why we went there in the first place. I was afraid of Him and loathed church.

• • •

I would always remember that incident, but eventually I forgot about my hateful words towards Jesus. Over time, my fears diminished and I actually began to enjoy Sunday school—though I still hated sitting through the sermons. I especially resented attending the evening service; there was always something on television I wanted to see.

One afternoon, when I was ten years old, I was thinking about the sinner's prayer. It dawned on me I had never said it. Immediately, I fell to my knees and asked Jesus into my heart. I acknowledged I was a sinner and dedicated my life to Him.

My parents, younger brother, and I then attended Christian Life Center, a large Assemblies of God church in Santa Rosa, California. We were there twice on Sundays, and on Wednesday nights I went to Royal Rangers. My parents enrolled me at the church's school when I started fifth grade, and I immediately fell behind in studies. The other kids discerned I was the class dunce, and some ridiculed me without pity. Whenever I was called up to the brown chalkboard to work out a math problem, a quiet snickering would last the entire time. The only friend I had at school was Steve Praetzel. During lunch, we told lame jokes and we spent several weekends at each other's house. He would go camping with my family, and I would bring the surplus army gear. At the campgrounds the two of us would storm the beaches of Normandy or fight off panzer tanks in the Ardennes. The following summer, Steve's parents joined YWAM (Youth With A Mission) and moved to a base in Austria. I would have to face sixth grade alone.

• • •

My baptism was on July 10 and I felt as clean as the day I accepted Christ as my Savior. However, the feeling did not last long. During that long, drought-stricken summer of 1977, some neighborhood friends and I would occasionally come across pornographic magazines in a nearby field while playing cowboys and Indians or army. Whatever we were playing, it was instantly forgotten when we found a dirty magazine. Looking through those glossy pictures did something to me. A sinister excitement grew within me.

• • •

Sixth grade was worse than fifth. I was either failing or below average in every subject. Some of the boys grew bored with merely teasing me. They found it fun to pretend to be my friend and then embarrass me in class by sharing something I told them in confidence. When it came to choosing teams at recess or PE, I was always the last one picked. My self-confidence hit rock bottom when I failed to advance to junior high. In order to cheer myself up, I set big goals for my future and told them to anyone who would listen.

Halfway through the next year, my parents transferred

me to Santa Rosa Christian School. Nobody there knew anything about me, and my grades improved with the easier curriculum. For the next two and half years I enjoyed being one of the popular kids at school. We were at that age where boys and girls begin noticing each other. It was frustrating, because the girls who liked me I wasn't interested in and the ones I liked were after somebody else. *No big deal, I'll get someone eventually,* I thought to myself.

In the summer of 1980, I went to Europe and spent six weeks with the Praetzels. Then my grandparents and I traveled throughout Austria, Switzerland, and Germany. In Berlin, I marveled at the sight of Russian tanks. I was fascinated with being on the frontlines of the cold war, and I loved the world travel.

A year later the Praetzels moved to Polson, Montana. My dad was fed up with the fast pace of California, so he moved our family there as well. It was a small town located on the south shore of Flathead Lake. The location was beautiful, but I felt out of place. My dad took to it like he was born there.

At the start of high school, I wanted another fresh beginning. But the school year had barely begun, and I was off to a bad start. I quit the freshman football team before our first game and I was already failing algebra. Yet, those things didn't matter as much to me as the fact that I really wanted a girlfriend. I had liked a lot of girls in junior high, but now I was serious about starting to date and longed for the prestige that came with having a girlfriend.

My parents had friends who had a daughter named Kelly. Over the summer I developed a huge crush on her, but Kelly had no interest in me. I saw her holding hands with some other boy at a Halloween party. The rejection crushed me, and that night I contemplated suicide for the first time. No matter how hard I tried, however, I could not deny the existence of heaven and hell. And deep within my soul I believed suicide victims were eternally separated from God. Could life on earth be worse than hell?

During my sophomore year, the Praetzels rejoined YWAM and moved to Salem, Oregon. Since Steve was no longer around, I became a life-long friend with Eric Lanes. That same year I met Kris and I was sure she was going to be my future wife. Kelly was soon forgotten. My only motivation for attending youth group and Sunday school was to be near this new girl.

The first time I asked her out, Kris politely made an excuse. The second time she gave me the familiar "Look, I only want to be friends" line. Capturing my heart was not enough, I thought; she had to crush it like a rotten tomato. While my parents were gone that night, I started playing with a .38 Special. I dumped out the rounds and dry fired it against the side of my head. Skin and hair capped the blue steel muzzle. My fingers dropped one bullet into a chamber. The cylinder was spun then slammed shut for a round of Russian roulette. I held the gun to my head for a minute, but chickened out. In an effort to get over Kris, I asked out several other girls, but they all declined. Each one just wanted "to be friends," but like a desert mirage they kept their distance from me.

I couldn't forget Kris, because she didn't avoid me. It was not beneath her to say hello or sit next to me on the bus. During my senior year I asked her for one of her school pictures. She obliged, and I kept it in my wallet. But looking at her picture was like antagonizing a festering wound.

•   •   •

Graduation was on a hot Sunday afternoon in May, and hundreds of people were packed into the school gymnasium for the ceremony. The girls wore pink and the boys wore

silver gowns. In an atmosphere of excitement, the Class of
'85 was about to step into the future. I only felt nervousness
and confusion. It appeared as if everyone else was about to
go off to college. My classmates had done their preparation
in advance. I had been so busy worrying about a girlfriend, I
had not given college any serious thought.

I spent that uncertain summer in Southern California,
half-heartedly looking for work and an affordable school.
When fall came around I ended up at a small community
college in Kalispell, a city about fifty miles north of Polson.
I was just killing time there. The next summer, I worked at a
salmon cannery in Petersburg, Alaska. After three months,
I managed to save enough money for a semester at Santa
Rosa Junior College.

• • •

The college had an excellent administration of justice (AJ)
program, which would help me with a career in law enforcement. I decided to study criminal justice for two years then
transfer to the college's police academy. On registration day
I was able to enroll in all of the classes I needed, but the
tuition cost me every dollar I made in Alaska. Afterwards,
I walked to the campus police office and applied for a job.
Four days later I was hired.

I was quickly accepted as one of the boys and invited
to every "choir practice" (our code words) for some serious
binge drinking. It felt good to be accepted, and I spent
many hours with my new friends at work, in class, and
at parties. Fortunately, because I worked weekend nights, I
missed most of the parties.

My work friends were good people, but they weren't
Christians. I wasn't attending church and hardly ever
prayed. At times I'd ask myself questions like, "What

happened to the boy who was on his knees asking Jesus into his heart? You know, the one who wore the 'King's Kids' T-shirt, and got baptized in front of that large congregation?" I missed that child, but he no longer existed.

My dorm roommate had a huge stack of pornographic magazines. I couldn't stay away from them. He often brought in X-rated videotapes. The movies were just fantasy; it was all sex without commitment or consequences. They gave me an urgent feeling that I was missing out on something. Almost everyone I knew at work was sexually active, and I felt inadequate, in my twenties and still a virgin. The pornography was like rat poison. Even though it was deadly to my spirit I craved more of it. Viewing those videos made me restless. I didn't just want to watch the action, I wanted to participate.

•   •   •

Quickly my days at the JC were coming to a close. In June 1988, the two-year AJ program would be completed and I would have to resign my job. There wasn't any money to put myself through the police academy, nor did I feel confident enough to complete it. I didn't want to become the aimless student I had been three years earlier, so for me there seemed to be no choice other than to enlist in the military. I wanted to see the world, so I chose the Navy.

On March 3, I drove to the Santa Rosa Federal Building. A vast lobby had one wall that sported a poster of an aircraft carrier sailing through a blue choppy sea. The caption said, "Take a World Cruise."

In the Navy office I was greeted by a first class petty officer named Sam McMakin. He was wearing dress blues with three red chevrons on the left sleeve. The office was decorated with small brass anchors and ships' bells. Blue carpet covered the floor. McMakin didn't have to give me the usual sales pitch about learning computer skills and earning college money.

"I'm sick of school," I told him, "I want to see the world and serve my country."

McMakin pointed to a world map on the wall covered with colored pins. "See that map? All of the orange pins are mine."

A black marine sergeant drinking from a red and yellow coffee mug walked over to the desk. He was solid as an oak. He pointed to a row of ribbons on his khaki shirt. "See this ribbon here? It's my Sea Service Ribbon. You'll be doing some traveling, believe me."

"Okay," I said to the petty officer, "let's do it."

A few days later, I returned to fill out a large stack of forms. On March 10, five high school seniors and I were loaded into a white van and driven to the MEPS (Military Entrance Processing Station) building in Oakland. That evening I took the ASVAB (Armed Services Vocational Aptitude Battery) test, which is the military's version of the SAT. Afterwards, the potential recruits were put up for the night in a low budget motel. I spent the whole next day going through a very thorough physical with a hundred other young men. All morning and most of the afternoon, every part of my body was poked, prodded, and analyzed by corpsmen and doctors. When the physical was completed, small groups of us were taken into a room to be sworn in by an Army captain. Before the swearing-in commenced, a staff sergeant made sure everyone had shirts tucked in and pants zipped.

By late afternoon we were sent to the counseling offices of our respective branches. The Navy office bustled like a large newsroom. People, desks, and noisy printers filled the bland interior. A detailer waved me over to his desk. He took my papers and typed up my contract on his computer. He didn't try to charm me like the recruiters in Santa Rosa had. In fifteen minutes he drafted a contract that basically said the U.S. Government would own me for the next four years. I took a deep breath and signed the dotted line.

When I returned to the campus I was walking on air, excited about the new adventures on my horizon. At the campus police office, I told the swing shift crew I would be building bombs and working on an aircraft carrier.

Then my excitement took a totally different direction when I discovered a note waiting for me from Caitlyn.

I had known Caitlyn seven years earlier at Santa Rosa Christian School. She had been one of those girls who liked me in junior high, but whom I had hardly noticed. I was still desperate for a girlfriend, so I looked her up, hoping the old spark was still burning. She was a student at the college. I left a note asking her to contact me. Much to my surprise she did. It took a couple of days for me to get the nerve to call her, but when she picked up the phone I was put at ease. She was flattered I had remembered her. I approached the subject of going out on a date with caution; I truly expected her to give me an excuse. When she accepted, I was at a loss for words. I had anticipated rejection, so I did not have anything planned. She asked if Friday night around seven was okay. It almost sounded as if she were asking me out.

Friday night came and she was everything I'd pictured her to be and more. She looked like Wynona Ryder. I kept asking myself why I hadn't paid attention to her in junior high. We went to a movie and back to my dorm room where we talked about the last seven years and people we knew from SRCS. I started thinking this just might work.

Unfortunately, I had to cut the date short. I had to be at work by midnight and was too dedicated to ask someone else to fill in for me. During our time together, I kept thinking of our next date, and the one after that, and when she would be hanging out in my room. While I drove her home, she kept talking about something which had happened to her recently. Then she added, ". . . that's when I was living with my boyfriend."

Those words killed the conversation, and neither of us said anything for several minutes. Words like "My ex-boyfriend" I could handle, but she said "boyfriend." When we got to her house I pretended I hadn't heard what she said.

"Are you seeing anyone?" I asked.

Caitlyn hesitated for a second. "Yeah, but I don't think it's going to last much longer. Call me on Monday, okay?"

I called on Monday. No answer. There was no answer all week. When she did finally pick up the phone she said what I had feared.

"I'm sorry, but I've been going out with this guy too long to just break up with him. We can still be friends, right?"

She starting talking about something else, but I didn't hear her. I just wanted to get off the phone; I don't even remember saying goodbye. It was even more painful than those rejections in high school. For the entire week I walked around campus like a zombie, hardly speaking to anyone. Much of my free time was spent drinking and watching pornographic videos in a vain attempt to ease the pain.

Two months later, I asked a girl named Stephanie if she would attend the campus police banquet with me.

"When is it again?" she asked.

"The Friday after next."

"Oh, I'm sorry, but I'll be out of town. How about my roommate Bonnie? She'd want to go."

I bought a new suit and went alone.

On June 10, I resigned from my job and left school. Now it was time to prepare for boot camp. I spent the summer in Montana running, swimming, weightlifting, and trying to forget about Caitlyn.

In August, I learned Kris was living in Kalispell. I decided to drive up and pay her a visit. She was still very pretty and I enjoyed our conversation until she mentioned her boyfriend. I began to notice that nearly every girl I spoke to, whether I was interested in her or not, would always slip in the "boyfriend" word, regardless of the topic. Years later I watched an episode of "Seinfeld" where one of the characters made the same observation. I picked up the hint, told her goodbye, and never saw her again.

For me, going into the Navy was like joining the French Foreign Legion. I wanted to leave everyone and every place I knew behind and travel to the far corners of the world. As I allowed the rejections of Caitlyn, Kris, and all the others to eat away at me, I began to come up with some distorted ideas. Marriage was nowhere to be seen in my future. My friend Eric and his wife Paula had been married two years, but I still couldn't get a girlfriend. I tried to convince myself a temporary artificial relationship was better than none at all.

At church, on the Sunday before I left for basic training, Pastor Finch asked if he could pray for me during the service. I agreed. He and some of the church board members laid hands on me. The pastor prayed for the Lord's protection upon me and asked that I might be a Christian witness to those with whom I would be serving. Something dark and sinister stirred within me as he spoke those words. As the presence of the Holy Spirit surrounded me, I felt exposed. If I needed God's help, I'd ask for it.

• • •

On the night of September 13 I sat in an old gray bus at the San Diego Airport. Fear of failure kept my perverted thoughts in check. But the other young men on board kept gawking at the women walking by. *These guys have got it bad*, I thought to myself. They kept acting like high school kids on a field trip until the first class petty officer returned and said, "Shut up! There's to be no talking."

It was a short ride from the airport to the Recruit Training Command. The only sounds were the bus's squeaky shocks and the passing traffic on Harbor Drive. Some guys were quietly laughing like it was all a big joke. I stared at the sunset on San Diego Bay and wondered how long I would last.

The bus stopped in front of the U-shaped R & O (Receiving and Outfitting) complex at Camp Nimitz. The petty officer got up from the driver's seat and in a thick Filipino accent said, "You've got thirty seconds to get off this bus and line up on the yellow feet painted outside."

The bus nearly fell apart as we rushed to get out. We stood abreast of each other breathing heavily. At a row of telephone booths, we were given two minutes to call home and tell our families we had arrived safely. The petty officer led us into a large forming room with a black and white tile floor. Inside were several very upset chief petty officers handing out small plastic cups. They were dressed in summer khakis and screamed obscenities. "Get in that head and fill up those cups, you dumb s---s!"

It was difficult to fill the cup while a salty chief yelled in my ear.

"What the hell you waiting for, boy? Fill it up!"

In another room, two old fat civilians gave us a ditty bag, a laundry bag, white socks, and PT (Physical Training) clothes. The two old men swore at us with the same proficiency as the chiefs. Two Company Commanders (Navy drill instructors) took us into the stencil room.

One CC slowly walked down an aisle while pointing

with his right arm extended. "Empty all your baggage and pockets onto the counters for inspection. What we leave, you keep; what we put in the garbage bags, you lose."

Rings, watches, and money were put into one white sock and placed into the front right pocket of our pants. Each of us was issued a thin mattress, a heavy gray wool blanket with "US" stenciled in black, and a pillow.

At midnight we were taken to the barracks. On a top bunk, I laid out my bedroll and climbed up. It was too hot to use the blanket, and sleep never came. Fear of the unknown gnawed at me. I looked out a window at two recruits standing watch by a Coke machine. Silently, I prayed for God's reassurance that I would make it through boot camp. After spending nearly every waking minute thinking about women, they were now the farthest thing from my mind. Even the perverted fantasies that I had taken such comfort in, could not alleviate my fears. Now that I was in a strange environment, I tossed aside those thoughts and turned to prayer.

At 5:00 A.M. the lights came on. "Get out of those racks! You're in the Navy now," boomed a voice. I expected to see a crusty old chief hurling a metal trashcan. Instead I saw senior recruits wearing faded blue dungarees and dingy gray leggings. Everyone was outside standing at attention in five minutes. Sweat ran down my face. We were then marched to the mess hall. Along the way we went over a wooden bridge that crossed a foul smelling salt-water canal separating Camp Nimitz from the rest of the RTC.

At the mess hall we were packed in like cattle. My face was buried in the hair of the guy in front of me. Metal trays and coffee mugs came straight out of the scullery, almost too hot to touch. But the hot trays at least gave some heat to the cold, liquid eggs and greasy bacon. Ten minutes after sitting at a table to eat, we were ordered to "Pop tall" and hurriedly ushered outside and formed into ranks on one of the grinders.

From the mess hall, we were marched to the barbershop, which had six chairs, each with a civilian barber dressed in a gold-colored smock. The barbers casually discussed the previous night's game between the Giants and Padres as their clippers sheared each recruit. When it was over, every recruit ran a hand over the top of his fuzzy head. In one minute my hair fell in a pile of brown locks on my lap.

After the haircuts, we were taken to the huge outfitting room. Each of us was handed a green sea bag made of canvas. In a single-file line we walked through a gauntlet of SKs (Store Keepers) who filled the sea bags with socks, gloves, underwear, T-shirts, jackets, swim trunks, white caps, dungarees, belts, and boondockers (black, steel-toed work shoes). After lunch, we were taken to the stenciling room where every item had to be marked with name and social security number.

The large group I had been with was divided into three companies. Ninety-seven of us were assigned to Company 226. While we were packing our sea bags, two company commanders walked into the room. One was a chief in khakis and the other was a Machinist Mate First Class in tropical whites. When we finished stenciling every item of clothing, the supervising petty officer turned to the CCs and said, "Okay, they're all yours."

The chief stepped onto a wooden pedestal and shouted, "Company two-two-six, attention!" We stood straight as possible, too scared to move. "My name is Chief Petty Officer Rodda, and this is Petty Officer Harris. We will be your company commanders for the duration of your basic training. You will end everything you say to us with 'Sir.' Do you understand?"

"Yes, Sir," the company asserted in unison.

"Bull s---! I still can't hear you," snapped the chief.

"YES, SIR!"

"That's better. Boot camp doesn't have to be difficult. In fact, it can be rather easy. Just do everything you're told to do, when you're told to do it, and the whole experience will be pretty simple."

• • •

When it came to weeding out the weaklings, the CCs didn't waste time. Seventeen days later, when the company was officially commissioned and transferred to the Division 8 Barracks, it was down to seventy-one recruits. Each day I feared I'd be the next to wash out. The fear of failure motivated me through every push-up. Mucus and sweat covered the barracks floor and soaked the uniforms while the push-ups increased in number. Rodda and Harris singled out certain recruits the way lions hunt weak wildebeest. Those who couldn't get with the program were harassed without mercy. Rodda was usually calm. He was of average height and build and would order us through grueling exercises with a velvet voice. Harris was five feet nine inches with a red mustache, a missing front tooth, and a wandering eye that made it difficult to tell who he was yelling at.

The days were spent marching, folding our clothes, and learning close-order drill with old M-1 rifles. If even one recruit messed up, we were all dropped for push-ups while the song, "Don't Worry, Be Happy" played from the CC's office. Those who struggled with the strict regimen were segregated to an area of the barracks called the "leper colony."

• • •

During those uncertain days of boot camp I found myself taking comfort in prayer and reading my green, pocket-size

New Testament. Through my own strength I tried to be a Christian, but I kept sinning in my thoughts and words. The perverted thoughts returned when I got back into my comfort zone. I never swore much prior to boot camp, but the constant bad language from everyone around me was contagious. However, despite my shortcomings, I experienced a miracle in the barracks.

I lost my swim trunks at R & O and got through two weeks without the CCs knowing. Then one afternoon they had each of us stand by our racks, so they could inspect our trunks. The company was scheduled for a swimming test the next day, and they wanted to make sure everyone had a pair. I panicked. Losing an article of clothing was a serious matter and would result in more than just a tongue lashing. The company stood in two lines facing each other from either side of the barracks. Each recruit was wearing blue gym shorts, white undershirts, shower shoes and holding a pair of trunks. As the CCs came closer, my pulse quickened, and I sent out a silent, but intense prayer. A cool ocean breeze blew through the open windows, but I could feel myself breaking into a sweat.

Suddenly, I heard someone speaking to me from my left, "Hey Porter." It was Herman Baca. "Are these yours?"

I looked over at him, and he was pointing to a pair of swim trunks on his rack. "No. Aren't they yours?"

"I've got mine right here." He held up another pair of tan trunks in his hand. "I don't know where these came from. They weren't there a minute ago."

I snatched up the extra pair and checked them. The initials inside weren't mine, but the trunks were my size. A couple of minutes later Harris came by and looked at the trunks then handed them back without a word. I was amazed. This was not a life or death situation, yet God intervened to keep me from being punished. If God is interested in my small problems, how much more interested is He in my major ones? I pondered the question for a while but eventually fell back into my old ways.

• • •

During service week most of us were assigned to the mess hall. We were lent out as laborers for the MSs (Mess Specialists) who were as ill tempered as the CCs. I slopped chow onto trays, hauled heavy boxes, and sweated in the scullery from 2:30 A.M. to 9:30 P.M. One evening after returning to the barracks, I found a letter on my rack. It was from a girl named Tracey. She'd been one of many I had asked out from the youth group in Polson. Tracey knew military boot camp could be a trying experience and she encouraged me to hang in there. I convinced myself she had an ulterior motive for writing. I couldn't wait to get home and give her a call.

Most of the recruits attended the Protestant chapel service on Sunday mornings. The services were held in a large auditorium where Lieutenant Commander Burt gave his motivating sermons. On our final Sunday the graduating companies were led into a smaller chapel, one with a large stained-glass window. The window pictured Jesus standing behind a sailor while He kept His hands on the helm of a storm-tossed ship. It was a simple message I failed to heed.

Graduation was Friday, 18 November 1988. Just before being released for our first liberty, Chief Rodda spoke to the company in the barracks. "I know all of you have been confined to the base for two and half months without any alcohol. Don't get stupid and try to make up for it in one weekend. You are not allowed to go to Tijuana. As for the hooks: Stay away from them! They're nothing but trouble in high-heels. And do you want to put a loaded gun to your head?"

A week later we packed our sea bags and filed out of the barracks for the last time. Company 226 was decommissioned and its members were sent to A-schools across the country. Those with aviation A-schools, such as myself, boarded a plane to Memphis.

2
NEW FRIENDS

The fear of the Lord is the beginning of knowledge, but fools despise wisdom and discipline. Proverbs 1:7

THE MEMPHIS NAVAL AIR STATION was located about thirty miles north of the airport in the city of Millington. I spent the first half of December on galley duty from 9 P.M. to 9 A.M. I worked in the mess hall with Ken Appler and Alan Bell, who had been in Company 227 in San Diego. We three would be attending the aviation ordnance school in January.

I was allowed two weeks leave for Christmas. While at home, I worked up my nerve to call Tracey. Since receiving her letter in boot camp, I convinced myself she was interested in going out with me. I had Bell read the letter and he said, "Oh yeah, this girl likes you. You should get with her when you go home."

Nervously I waited for her to pick up the phone. She answered and we exchanged the usual small talk. Then I asked if she'd be free to do something that week. After an awkward silence she said, "Well, I really can't. I'm seeing someone."

I wasn't disappointed this time, since I'd prepared myself for such a response. Each perceived rejection provided another excuse to justify an illicit lifestyle. Soon that lifestyle would take hold.

I didn't have to be back to the base until January 3, but the latest flight I could get was on New Year's Eve. Not wanting to spend my last days of leave sitting around the barracks, I got a motel room near the Memphis airport. When evening arrived, I put on my dress blues and started walking towards a bar to see in the new year. I hadn't gone far when a pale green van pulled alongside me. Inside sat a skinny white dude with a bad haircut—short in front and long in back. Sitting beside him, his girlfriend wore faded jeans and a gray sweatshirt. They looked as if they both lived in some rundown trailer with half a dozen bloodhounds.

"You wanna date?" the girl asked with a Southern accent.

I knew what she was asking and automatically accepted her offer.

"You got a room where we can go?" she asked.

I pointed towards the motel. "Yeah, it's right over there."

"Hop in, buddy. We'll give you a ride over there," the driver said.

They must have seen my apprehensive look, because the girl said, "It'll be all right, honey. We're not gonna hurt you."

I climbed into the van, leaving all caution at the curb. The girl moved over to give me room. On the way to the motel she quoted her price and I agreed. When we got there, I was so nervous I had trouble unlocking the door.

"Are you sure you've got the right key?"

"Yeah, there's only one."

Inside the room she took my money and said, "My name's Loretta. What's yours?"

"Jake."

While taking off her sweatshirt she said, "I don't usually do this, you know. It's just that things are tough at home, and I've got kids to support. You understand, right?"

"Yeah, sure."

"I hate to rush you, dear, but there's someplace I have to be in thirty minutes so we'll have to hurry."

When it was over, and she had taken my money, she rushed out the door and jumped into the van, which sped off down the busy street. My head was spinning. Overcome with shame, I dropped to my knees and asked God to forgive me.

I spent the next day in my room watching TV. About 11:00 A.M. a black maid came to the door and asked, "Does your room need to be cleaned?"

"No."

A couple of hours later she returned and asked the same question.

"No, everything's fine."

That evening, she came by again, but this time she wasn't in uniform.

"Can I use your bathroom?" she asked.

I let her in. She came out of the bathroom and began undressing. "You want some company?"

"Yeah, sure." I hesitated. "But I haven't got any money."

"Not any?"

"None."

She thought for a minute then said, "That's okay. We can still have a good time."

She stayed about fifteen minutes. Eventually, I asked her to leave, but not before things had gone too far. I found myself reciting the same prayer of less than twenty-four hours earlier. This time it rang hollow.

• • •

On January 3 my roommate, Adam Price, and I were assigned to AOA class 89062, which was a night class with eighteen sailors and six Marines. The first week was called EBAT (Enlisted Basic Aviation Training) in which we learned the physics of flight. After EBAT, the actual training for aviation ordnance began. Phase one consisted of learning about the support equipment known as yellow gear, and phase two covered every aspect of Navy air delivered weapons. We learned about bombs, missiles, rockets, mines, and electrically-powered Gatling guns.

The AO School had an interesting group of instructors and each one taught a particular subject. For a week we had Staff Sergeant Bradley who was so sickened by the sailors' lack of discipline he made us drill and double time around the grinder before class. Then there was AO1 Rote who had been in the Navy since Vietnam and was mad at the world because he couldn't get promoted.

AO1 Silks was a loud, foul-mouthed hillbilly from Appalachia. During personnel inspections he'd chastise any student who was putting on weight while his own beer belly drooped past his belt buckle. When the topic of the evening had been covered and there was time to spare, Silks would tell sea stories. The most interesting ones were of his sexual exploits in foreign ports. His vocabulary became more graphic and his voice louder while recalling his past ventures. I had difficulty believing this was taking place in a classroom instead of a barracks.

On a Saturday afternoon, I was just outside the North gate when two men approached me. They asked if I knew Jesus Christ and would I be interested in attending their church in Memphis. Reluctantly, I answered yes to both questions. They told me the church would be sending a shuttle to the base in the morning.

Early the next morning I put on my winter blues (also called a Johnny Cash suit) and boarded the shuttle with several other sailors for the drive to Memphis. We were taken to the Bellevue Baptist Church, and it looked similar to Christian Life Center (now Luther Burbank Center for the Arts) in Santa Rosa, but even bigger.

After the service, all the sailors and marines were ushered into the church's recreation facility, which included a bowling alley. There was nothing there that interested me, but I didn't want to leave the impression I was ungrateful for what they were trying to do. I found a place to sit down and sipped coffee from a Styrofoam cup. Several church volunteers spread out amongst the servicemen and witnessed to them on an individual basis. Before long, a middle-aged woman sat next to me.

"Hello, what's your name?" she asked.

"Jake."

"Jake, do you know what it means to be a Christian?"

I tried to recall the definition from the back of my memory and said, "Yes. A person asks Jesus to come into his heart and to take control of his life."

The look on her face showed she was surprised by my answer. "Then are you a Christian?"

"Yes I am," I said confidently.

The woman and I talked for a few more minutes, then she excused herself to go witness to someone else. One part of me wanted to run away, but another wanted to stay and somehow reunite with my Christian past. I'd never been in that church before, yet it seemed familiar. There'd been something missing in my life far too long.

•   •   •

On a Friday night Appler, Bell and I caught a cab into Memphis where each of us rented a motel room for the weekend. My plan was to take them to a nude dancing bar and then go to some blues club on Beale Street the next day. We stayed at the same motel where I had spent New Years. We made it to the girlie bar and the manager let us in even though my friends were underage. This manager looked like a real scumbag. His wardrobe was something left over from the disco era and he combed his hair like Elvis Presley. The wide tip collar of his shirt overlapped the one on his brown leather jacket. His looks were topped off with gold chain necklaces and mutton-chop sideburns that would have made the king proud. Dollar signs popped up in his eyes at the sight of our uniforms.

Inside, the place was totally dark except for neon strobe lights highlighting the dancers on stage and amplified speakers thumping out loud rock music. The dancers and cocktail waitresses were money sharks. Elvis probably didn't pay his girls much, so they depended on fleecing the customers. It didn't take long to figure out what this place was all about since they charged $3.50 for a bottle of beer. Any other place would have charged $1.25.

A brunette dancer wearing a red bikini and high heels came over to us and shouted over the music, "Hi, my name is Mindy. I offer table dances for ten dollars and lap dances for twenty."

This went on the entire evening, and I held on to my wallet while being transfixed by the dancers. After four hours my friends were flat broke. In the morning, they returned to the base while I stayed at the motel. Instead of going out for some blues music and barbeque, I held on to my money and returned to the club when it got dark. The place had me hooked.

• • •

During our training, each man wondered where he would be stationed. Most were hoping for a shore duty billet. Silks angrily asked the students why they joined the Navy if they did not want sea duty. No one answered him. We were allowed to choose our orders on March 1. The school's head instructor, AOC Allen, walked into the classroom and began writing on the chalkboard.

The chief made a list of the duty stations and how many billets were available for each. There were openings for air stations, squadrons, and ship's company. None of the duty stations appealed to me, because they were all on the East Coast. When my turn came to choose, there were only ship's company billets, so I selected the USS America in Norfolk, Virginia. While returning to the barracks, I began to have second thoughts. Silks, the barracks petty officer that evening, asked each student about his orders.

"What did you get, Porter?"

"The America."

Silks let out a loud laugh. "You remember when I told you all about the time I spent over a hundred days at sea?"

"Yeah."

"Well that was on the America. Price's goin' there with ya'. You two are gonna have a great time. That boat's a sea-goin' mother ------."

Luis Carbonana, a student in our class, had his orders to Sigonella, Sicily changed to duty on the America, because he took an unauthorized sick day.

"Can you believe the captain did that?" Price asked me during a break.

"Interesting, isn't it? The Navy sends people to the America as punishment," I said.

Graduation was held in the AO hangar on March 15, 1989. When the ceremony concluded we were dismissed to start the lengthy check out process and to go to the personnel office for our orders. I was to report aboard the America on April 3.

• • •

Before going to Norfolk I had two weeks leave. In Polson, snow and ice still covered the ground. On my first night back I paid a visit to the apartment of my friend Eric and his wife Paula. My friend Tommy was there, and Eric's two little girls were running wild. Everyone was surprised to see me.

"He heard that Kris is getting married and he's come back to rescue her," said Paula.

They all laughed. I forced a smile, but felt as if I had just been kicked in the teeth. When I had seen her the summer before I accepted the fact she was out of my life forever, but it was still painful news.

My stomach was in knots during the flight to the East Coast. I was not sure how I was going to find a ship at a large, unfamiliar base in the middle of the night. While waiting for the last leg of my journey in Pittsburgh, a petty officer came over to where I was sitting and asked if I was going to Norfolk for the first time. There were several sailors waiting for the flight, but I was the only one in uniform and carrying a large brown envelope.

"Yeah, I am. But, I have no idea how to get to my ship," I answered.

"What ship are you going to?"

I told him.

"I think the America is at pier eleven. When we arrive in Norfolk I'll make sure you get to the personnel office."

The plane landed in Norfolk shortly before midnight. In the airport terminal was a large illuminated picture of Pat Robertson. The sign invited people to the CBN studios in Virginia Beach to watch a broadcast of "The 700 Club." As a child I had watched the show with my mother before going to school. Once again I felt much as I had at the church in Memphis, longing to get in touch with my Christian past.

Outside, in front of the luggage area, most of the sailors climbed into a shuttle going to the base. When we arrived, the helpful petty officer made sure the driver got me to the base personnel office. I thanked him, then carried my heavy sea bag up the steps into the red brick building. The PNs (Personnelmen) told me the America would return to Norfolk in two days. In the mean time, I was to stay in the transient barracks.

An FA (Fireman Apprentice) and I had the entire third

deck of the barracks to ourselves. Nobody had been there in years. A large sheet of dried paint, attached to the ceiling, hung about four feet from the floor. Smaller chips covered the floor's green tile, and dust clung to the windowsills. I climbed into a rack and slept until late morning.

When I awoke, I put on my winter blues. The FA and I went to chow and walked along the piers where the giant gray ships were moored. Nearly every building was made of red bricks with white doors. As we walked away from a pier where several destroyers were moored, a gray Honda Civic stopped in front of us. Inside were two attractive Asian girls who waved us over. The passenger handed us each a business card. Before either of us could read it the car sped off. The card was advertising a Japanese massage parlor in Virginia Beach. The FA threw his away, but I stuck mine into my shirt pocket. There was nothing on the card to suggest there was anything besides a massage, but something inside me knew it was not a legitimate business.

The next day I met up with three guys I knew from A-school, Luis Carbonana, Adam Price, and Larry Watkins. Watkins had been majoring in computer science at a college in Indiana when he dropped out to join the Navy. That evening we went to Trade Winds, which was one of the base e-clubs. Over glasses of beer, we discussed the rumor that had been circulating around the barracks. In May, the America would be leaving for a six-month Mediterranean cruise.

"Man, a six-month Med cruise already. I can't believe it," said Price staring into his glass.

"I'm not ready for this. I was hoping to get to Indiana and see my daughter," said Watkins.

My companions were feeling down, but I was ecstatic. It meant I would be indulging my pent up lust sooner than expected.

There were over fifty men in the transient barracks, and

except for a few, all were going to the America. Their ranks ranged from first class petty officers down to recruits and were made up of nearly every rate. The following morning everyone put on dress blues and packed their sea bags. When my friends and I made it to the pier I was awestruck. The ship was massive, and I had to bend my back to see the blue union jack flapping on the bow. On the starboard side of the tower was a white 66. Across the pier was the USS John F. Kennedy. The two carriers formed a type of wind tunnel that nearly blew my cap into the river.

At the top of the after brow, a chief took our orders and said, "Welcome aboard." Turning to the duty seaman he ordered, "Take these men to the personnel office!"

Walking through the hangar bay was like entering the belly of a giant metallic beast. It stretched from the fantail to the forecastle and was twenty-four feet high. Heavy steel watertight doors lined the portside. The personnel office was a beehive of activity, and the nearby crew's lounge was crowded with new arrivals waiting for the PNs to process their orders. After several hours, someone from the weapons department took us to the berthing compartment and assigned us racks and lockers. We were told to go back to the personnel office in four days. Four days off would've been great, but my paycheck was still in Memphis. Except for those on duty, the entire crew was on liberty.

When we returned to the personnel office they took our papers and sent us up to the weapons department office on the 03 level. Inside there was a fat master chief sitting behind a desk, while two airmen office workers filed papers.

"Wilson, bring me their orders!" said the master chief.

A short office worker in pressed dungarees took our brown envelopes and gave them to his boss. The master chief took several minutes to read our orders. Finally he spoke again to Wilson. "Send Carbonana to G-3 and the others to G-1."

A black petty officer led Price, Watkins, and me to the main G-1 shop. We went back down to the hangar bay, walked aft, and climbed up through a scuttle. In the space, forty-five pairs of eyes stared at us. Petty officers and airmen sat or stood together smoking and watching MTV. Most of them were younger than I, but they were salts with a glassy look in their eyes. They wore blue ship's-ball caps, faded dungarees, flight-deck boots, and green foul-weather jackets.

A first class walked up to me and extended his hand. "I'm Petty Officer Wilder."

I shook his hand but was too nervous to say anything.

"Can you talk?" Wilder asked. He was from Rhode Island, but he looked like a cowboy.

"Yeah, I can talk. I'm Jake Porter."

Wilder introduced me to several of the airmen who hardly acknowledged me. There were Jason Spells and Darren Stinson from Arkansas, Brad Cullen and Chris Soukup from the Dakotas, and sleeping on top of a metal cabinet was a grungy little West Virginia hillbilly called "Froggy." He got his nickname because he talked like a character from the old "Our Gang" series. He may have sounded like a frog, but he hated water. He wore the same oily dungarees every day and never showered.

There was a nut named Preston Marks who was so psychologically unsound he thought he could turn himself invisible, and he told people he was a CIA operative. He was dead serious and cussed a blue streak at any derision. There was Justin Sprague from Sarasota, Florida, Kevin Langkam from Maryland, Kevin Kelleher from Hollywood, Ralph Prisco from New York City, and Paul Whorely from Georgia. There were three different guys named Smith and all were called "Smitty," including the LPO (Leading Petty Officer).

There was nothing much to do, so we watched MTV until the LPO dismissed us. After dismissal, Price and I went to the ship's store to buy ball caps. Only new arrivals wore white caps with dungarees and we didn't want to stand out. More people showed up the following week and I became close friends with three of them—Manuel Pena from Las Cruces, New Mexico, Scott Straub from Columbus, Ohio, and Wil Diaz of Miami.

G-1 was divided into five work centers; the flight deck center operated independently and did not muster with us in the morning. All the new guys were assigned to the hangar deck work center, where the most people were needed and the hardest work was required.

A week after reporting on board I saw four G-1 members standing in front of the base theater. I got a can of orange soda and stood with them and listened to their conversation. The ship had just returned from France, and they were talking about a Paris brothel. They were not ashamed, and each of them had steady girlfriends back in their hometowns. They laughed and bragged about their exploits.

My mind contemplated the possibilities overseas. I remembered what I had told myself in college when my anticipated relationship with Caitlyn failed: If I could not have a relationship with a woman, then a temporary encounter would suffice. A brothel would be perfect, especially in a country where nobody knew me, and there would be no condemnation from my peers. The prayers for forgiveness in Memphis were forgotten.

The business card for the Japanese massage parlor had been in my wallet for a couple of weeks. I should have thrown it away, but didn't, or couldn't. An inner turmoil raged within me. I wanted sex, but did not want to go before the Lord again and ask for forgiveness. However, after a pitcher of beer at Trade Winds, I persuaded Price and Carbonana to go with me to the massage parlor. We hailed a taxi, which took us to Virginia Beach. The place was easy to find and the nearby residential area lent it some respectability. The lobby looked

like the waiting room of a doctor's office, with back issues
of Time and Newsweek lying on a rectangular coffee table
and anatomy charts hanging on the white walls. After a few
minutes a lady came to the receptionist window. After taking
our money she led us to separate rooms. The lady stayed with
me, while two others were assigned to my companions. I was
not disappointed.

A few days before the ship was to set sail, the division
had a barbeque at a park in Virginia Beach. Petty officers and
airmen wearing shorts, T-shirts and sunglasses sat on the picnic
tables drinking beer and eating hamburgers. Gunner Weaver
(the division officer) and Chief Webb brought their families.
Froggy and the chief's son tossed a baseball back and forth. As
the beer flowed, some of the senior petty officers began telling
sea stories from years past. Once again I found myself listening
to tales about various brothels around the world. These were
not confused eighteen-year-olds just out of high school, they
were grown men with wives and families.

When Wilder finished one of his stories, he looked at Price
and me and said, "When you're part of the fleet you share
everything with each other. And yes, sometimes that includes
our women as well."

"Does that include your wife?" asked Cullen.

Wilder looked at him hard with blood shot eyes. "Don't
be a smart ass."

Everyone laughed.

What Christian values I had left would never be able to
withstand such strong temptations, so I did not make an effort
to resist. Even our leaders, the ones we looked up to, were
encouraging immoral behavior.

• • •

On May 11, gray tugboats pulled the America away from its
pier and into the mouth of the James River. A cold wind blew.

Under an overcast sky a twin rotor UH-46D helicopter flew off the portside and stayed with the ship as it entered the choppy green water of Chesapeake Bay.

Since I had to work night check from 7 P.M. to 7 A.M., I went to my rack. When I awoke, the ship was in the Atlantic Ocean. The strong wind blew through the open, massive aircraft elevator doors on the starboard side of the hangar bay. Across the sapphire blue water no land was in sight. Planes landed on the flight deck overhead, bringing the squadrons aboard. Heavy tail hooks pounded the steel deck followed by the loud screeching of arresting cables.

I was ambushed inside the shop. Two of the bigger sailors threw me to the deck while somebody else ripped open my shirt. Buttons flew off like popcorn kernels. My T-shirt was lifted and everyone took turns slapping my bare stomach with open hands. It was my first day at sea, so I was "dogged." When the next new guy popped up the scuttle, the same thing happened to him.

My work center supervisor was AO1 Bill Crawford. He was a solid farm boy from Georgia, and he didn't say anything about my open shirt. He handed me three red, long-sleeved jerseys, a "G-1" stencil, and a can of black spray paint. "Put one of these on after you stencil the front and back," he said with a heavy southern accent through a mouthful of tobacco.

Crawford was a good supervisor. He let us watch television when there was nothing to do, but made everyone go on deck when ordnance was to be moved. If there was idle time he made sure the new people were studying for their damage control and 3M (maintenance and material management) qualifications.

On the second evening I was reading a letter from home when a JP-5 (aviation fuel) pump exploded, killed two men, and spread fire on three decks.

The 1MC (the ship-wide public address system)

announced, "On board the America, Fire! Fire! Fire! All hands man your battle stations. Damage control set condition zebra throughout the ship." Condition zebra meant all watertight doors and hatches were to be sealed. G-1's battle station was the bomb farm, the staging area for ordnance being sent to the flight deck. Smoke was drifting through the hangar deck, and damage control men were running everywhere. The hangar bay was now full of aircraft with wings folded back and chalking chains attached to their wheels.

Three hours later the fire was extinguished, and we went back to work as if nothing happened. I didn't know the two who were killed, but it was the first time any co-workers of mine had died instantly on the job. I began to think, *If I die, will I go to Heaven?* Had I been forgiven for those salacious encounters? I had repented of those sins, but had ever since longed for a repeat of the experiences. There were times I chastised myself for asking that maid to leave. Pornography was always available. Centerfolds were taped to the bulkhead of the yellow gear storage area above the bomb farm. Marks tended to the care of those pictures like it was his assigned duty. He nearly cried when the gun boss ordered them to be taken down.

At times the work was almost overbearing. During my first weapons on load we worked for two days with little food and no sleep. Chief Webb did not allow anyone to sleep until the magazines were filled with the hundreds of bombs the ammunition ship was sending over. The days began to blend into each other and Sunday was no different than Wednesday.

The only break we received from the mundane and tiring work came during mail call. Mail was like gold. Everyone, officer and enlisted, stopped what he was doing and tore open any letter with his name on it. I enjoyed the letters from home, but I was envious of those who were getting perfume-scented envelopes. Often they contained pictures of the girlfriends or wives who sent them; and they would make the rounds. It only reminded me of what I had been denied; and it was something they took for granted.

One afternoon, I walked out onto a sponson next to the division AWSEP (Aviation Weapons Support Equipment Program) shop. Standing in front of the ship's whaleboat I leaned on the rusty railing and looked out to sea. The ship was halfway across the Atlantic. I often went there for privacy, which was hard to find. As the wind swirled around the sponson, I thought about how nice it would be to receive a letter from a girl back home.

I opened my wallet and took out the picture of Kris I'd been carrying for four years. I stared at it a long time. It wasn't just a picture of some girl I once had a crush on. It represented the wholesome image of the girl next door. She seemed like the kind of girl a guy was supposed to marry after high school and live with happily-ever-after in their new home with a two-car garage. *Right now, another man is doing just that. It's the type of situation my parents walked into. So what is wrong with me?* I decided to reject society's precedent of proper courtship and God's ordinances concerning morality. I had convinced myself it was impossible for me to ever marry and that brief encounters with prostitutes would be the only kind of relationship I could hope for. Reluctantly, I released the picture and watched the wind carry it into the waves.

3
THE MED

Furthermore, since they did not think it worthwhile to retain the knowledge of God, He gave them over to a depraved mind, to do what ought not to be done. Romans 1:28

TEN DAYS OUT TO SEA, we spotted the Azores to the north. The islands glistened like emeralds set on blue velvet and surrounded by mist. At 4:00 A.M. on May 24 I saw the lights of Tangier, Morocco off the starboard bow as the ship entered the Strait of Gibraltar. Four recruits from G-3 stood "monkey watch." It was a joke played on new arrivals fresh out of boot camp. They wore red helmets and carried billy clubs to whack any monkey that swam from shore.

As daylight dawned, the Rock of Gibraltar came into view. On the other side, sleepy Arab villages sat on water's edge. After quarters, I hit my rack and thought about finally experiencing liberty in a foreign port. Two hours later the ship anchored at Benidorm, Spain.

I had barely got to sleep when the boatswain's whistle blew and liberty call was announced. Pena and I changed into civilian clothes and stood in the long line forming on the hangar deck. Manuel Pena was a tall American Indian who spoke fluent Spanish. Wil Diaz called him "Chief" because he looked similar to the Indian character in *One Flew Over the Cuckoo's Nest.*

After arriving at fleet landing, Pena and I went to a café and drank beer while looking at the Mediterranean Sea. Benidorm, a resort city, has numerous high-rise hotels and is surrounded by white cliffs. European tourists strolled along its narrow streets and sandy beachfront.

In the afternoon we met up with other guys from the division. The small group became a pack of intoxicated AOs with Crawford leading the way. Once, as we left a bar Crawford said, "Hey, let's go to a whorehouse."

I was all for it, and said, "Let's go."

The others laughed. Crawford looked at me and smiled with bits of tobacco sticking to his teeth. "I was only kidding, Porter. I'm gonna have to keep my eye on you."

The division mustered in the main shop at 6:00 A.M. in dungarees and ball caps. The mustering was to make sure everyone was accounted for, and after an hour the chief dismissed those not in the duty section. When I started to leave the shop Airman Pete Castille stopped me.

"Were you serious about going to a whorehouse?"

"Yeah," I answered.

"Well I went to one last night after leaving you guys. You want to know where it's at?"

"Sure."

He gave me directions on how to get to the place from fleet landing. That morning I went ashore by myself and set out for the brothel. It was exactly where Castille said it would be, across the street from the building with the giant soccer ball on top. The arched doorway to the place was covered with a heavy purple curtain. Pushing the curtain aside, I stepped in and let my eyes adjust to the darkness. My heart pounded hard. I could hear it in my head.

I came to the end of a small bar. Two sad-looking women, wearing black lingerie and smoking cigarettes, sat at the opposite end. They ignored me. An overweight woman with heavy makeup and an artificial fur stole walked over to me. "May I get you something?" She forced a smile.

I sat on a stool and ordered a beer. The madam handed me a bottle and went over to where the two women were sitting. She tried to get one of them to sit next to me, but neither wanted to. My nervousness had not been calmed, and it was obvious I was not wanted there. I guzzled down the beer then stood up. The madam started towards me, but I quickly left before she could say anything.

What's wrong with you? I asked myself. *Do you want to do this or not?*

I met up with Crawford and the gang that afternoon. Castille was with them. "Hey Porter, did you find that place?"

"Yeah, but I didn't do anything."

We were sitting at a table outside a café. He leaned his skinny body forward and asked, "Why not?'

"I don't know."

"I think I'll go back there tonight. You want to come with me?"

"No, that's all right." I felt confused and wished he would change the subject.

He had a Christian upbringing and was a dropout from a Southern California community college. "I've had all kinds of whores and some I didn't even have to pay for," he bragged while brushing away a lock of his greasy black hair.

The group jeered him. Spells said, "Shut up, Castille."

A smile crossed his gaunt face. "Hey, I don't care if you guys believe me or not. Porter, you're sure you don't want to go there with me?"

"No, I'm fine."

Crawford focused his watery red eyes on me and asked, "Porter, how come you're not drinking?"

"I don't know. I guess I don't feel like it."

"Bull s---." Crawford slapped some money down on the

table. "Waiter, get this man a beer."

During our last night in Benidorm, Wil and I were invited to a British pub where there was an X-rated magic show. The place was packed with sailors from the ship. During the show, the bartender continued cleaning glasses like nothing was out of the ordinary. Afterwards, everyone headed back to the ship. From the outside the resort city gave no trace of the seedy entertainment available there. The tourists kept window-shopping and drinking fruit-flavored daiquiris.

Back at the ship, night check had to report for duty because we were pulling out in the morning. I put on my dungarees and climbed up the ladder into the shop. Crawford slumped over his desk, sleeping one off. I found a seat and watched television until morning when day check arrived.

• • •

While at sea, the long days of hard work continued without let-up. Tempers grew short, and some people enjoyed making the miserable experience worse for others. Abuse of power was a common practice. A supervisor would push his men to the breaking point and hope one of them would backtalk. When one did talk back it provided the excuse he needed to send the man to captain's mast. And the captain always sided with the superior in a dispute.

AO3 Stewart disdained the airmen even more than the chiefs did. Stewart was one of those retreads who left the Navy then came back when he couldn't get a civilian job. With narrow green eyes beneath a freckled forehead he glared at his subordinates. He was fond of saying, "That's a direct order." Whenever that phrase followed a command it meant the person it was directed at was a breath away from captain's mast. It was said rarely by most petty officers, but Stewart drew it like a gun.

Being the lowest rank in the Navy was tough enough, but

dealing with self-aggrandizing dictators was too much. I hated the Navy and wanted out. World travel no longer appealed to me. Everything I tried in life seemed to backfire on me. This was something I had volunteered for and there was no one to blame but me. I went out to the sponson, sat on a low platform beneath the whaleboat, and took from my pocket a small razor. Dreams of suicide haunted me more than ever, but I could never actually do the deed. *Maybe if I attempt it they will give me a medical discharge on a section eight. It's worth a try.*

I held the small razor with two fingers and I tried to cut my left wrist, but it was dull. I tossed the blade into the water and silently cried out to God. As soon as the tears formed in my eyes I wiped them away, in case someone from AWSEP should see me. *Oh God, please help me*, I silently prayed. Strangely, I did begin to feel an inner peace. And I didn't have any conflict with Stewart after that.

Airman Lee Fuller nearly wrapped a chalking chain around Stewart's skull one afternoon. Fuller was a lot smaller, but he wasn't afraid of anyone. He swore and said, "I'm gonna bash your brains out," while swinging the heavy chain and hook.

Stewart ran to division and put Fuller on report. Gunner kept the incident in-house. It was an answered prayer for me, because Stewart quit hassling everyone.

The ship's next port-of-call was Palma, an old city of Renaissance architecture on the island of Mallorca. It was a primary anchorage in the Mediterranean for the Sixth Fleet. There were a lot of English pubs and cafes, but every sailor ate at Texas Jack's or the USO.

I spent the first day with Manuel Pena walking around the downtown area. That evening, we went into a large bar that was crowded with sailors. Two cocktail waitresses busily served drinks to the rowdy mob. One was quite attractive, but the other was really overweight. They both wore lingerie and tried to serve drinks while being pinched and groped.

"Hey, some guys were saying those waitresses are for sale, if you're interested," Pena told me.

I was very interested. When the pretty one walked by I stopped her and asked, "How much?"

Pena translated. When she answered, a look of shock came across his face. "She costs twenty-thousand pesetas."

That came to about a hundred-fifty dollars. "Hey Mannie, loan me fifty bucks," I said.

Reluctantly, Pena handed me a large wad of multi-colored paper pesetas.

I was scared to death, but I made myself go through with it. The waitress took all my cash and had me follow her. All the other sailors cheered and hooted as the girl led me into a back room. I felt as if the whole world were witnessing me cross the line into deliberate sin.

The bedroom she took me to was right next to the barroom where the rowdy sailors were. Only paper-thin walls separated the rooms. She pointed to her cheap gold watch, indicating I had ten minutes; there were other paying customers. She kept pointing to that watch the whole time and saying, "Prisa para arriba!"

When it was over she hurried back to the bar area and resumed her waitress duties. The crowd cheered. As Manuel and I left the bar I looked over at the girl to wave goodbye. She glanced over at us, but did not acknowledge me. I was just another opportunist.

The excitement of a temporary relationship was missing. *Isn't a brief sexual encounter supposed to be better than no relationship at all?* I asked myself. The girl did not even wave good-bye and it hurt as much as any rejection I had experienced in school.

That night I tried to fall asleep, but I felt the same familiar depression. I felt alone and empty. Jesus had been evicted from my life. I had deliberately committed a sin of immorality and now there was no one to turn to when trouble arose. I tried asking God for forgiveness, but I still felt dirty. The cruise had just gotten underway, and there would be plenty of other temptations, temptations that would be too strong for a sinner to overcome.

•   •   •

At Izmir, Turkey, a local ferryboat carried the group I was with from the ship into the harbor. At fleet landing, it tied up alongside a fishing boat, which we had to walk across in order to reach the pier. On the streets a foreigner could not walk ten feet without a shine boy wanting to polish his shoes. Most refused, because they wore Nikes or other running shoes. The boys didn't care; they only wanted the dollar they charged. They'd say, "Ah, give me a break, it's my birthday."

In Izmir, a maze of alleys divided ancient buildings. Inside dark cafés, men in caftans and fezzes drank tea and smoked water pipes. Throughout the day, followers of Islam would go to the mosque, remove their shoes, and prostrate themselves on prayer rugs. Women were not allowed in public unless accompanied by their husbands or fathers, and we were forbidden to speak with them.

In most major cities of Turkey there is an area called the "Compound." The Compound is a segregated area where the city's prostitutes are allowed to work. Every woman there has a husband in prison. A prisoner can have his sentence reduced or suspended by paying the courts a large sum of money. Often, the only way he can raise the money is to have his wife work as a prostitute under government supervision.

Several members of G-1 went to Izmir's Compound and later described it to me. Inside a walled-off area there were four narrow streets lined with small houses, and in front of each house were four or five women wearing bathing suits.

Night check hangar deck and forklift personnel met in the main shop while the ship weighed anchor and turned south.

"Hey, did any of you guys go to the Compound?" asked Justin Sprague. He was a scrawny airman with wiry brown hair.

"Yeah," chorused several voices.

"They were so ugly I turned around and left," said Sprague.

From where he was seated at his desk, Crawford volunteered, "I had a cute one—"

"I left too," Cullen interrupted. "But that one in the green wasn't . . . Hey! What's Marks doing behind those boxes?"

"You guys aren't suppose to see him; he's invisible," said Spells.

"—You all want to hear this or not?" asked Crawford, slightly irritated. Normally he was strictly business in the work place, but he wasn't quite sober yet. "She was a little thing and kept squirmin' to get away. So, I had to slap her around a bit." He laughed.

"You went to the Compound? You're married," I reminded him.

"I'm only married in the States."

• • •

The America made its way south and on June 24 anchored off Port Said, Egypt. The surrounding water was a vast parking lot for ships. Each one waited its turn to enter the Suez Canal. When the carrier made its slow journey through the desert, the sun beat down on the steel flight deck, and the giant aircraft elevators of the hangar bay were sealed shut. Only the machinist's mates and cooks had to work.

The west bank of the canal sported many lush oases with date trees and vacation resorts. The east side offered nothing but the endless sand dunes of the Sinai wilderness. In the intense heat, the flight deck's non-skid smelled like fresh tar.

Eventually, the green to the west gave way to harsh desert as well. By late afternoon the ship reached the end of the canal. A battered wooden fishing boat straddled the Sinai Desert and the sea.

When night fell, it was back to work. It would be a long time before we hit another port. The heat and humidity of the Red Sea was the worst I had ever endured. The ship's air conditioning was useless against the hot sticky air, and sleep was impossible.

A week later the ship entered the Indian Ocean. The closer we got to the equator, the hotter it became. Warm mist hovered above the surface of the green water as if we were sailing across a giant bowl of soup. The humidity was visible in the hangar bay, and the heat sapped everyone's energy.

After the ship crossed the equator, the climate cooled. We were now where it was winter. After reaching the vicinity of Diego Garcia, the ship circled the tiny island for three weeks. Every day was the same. In G-1 we were constantly breaking out yellow gear or putting it back into storage. My conscience had numbed since Palma. Girlie magazines were plentiful, and I was ready to act out my perverted thoughts in Singapore.

4

INTO THE QUAGMIRE

All at once he followed her like an ox going to the slaughter, like a deer stepping into a noose till an arrow pierces his liver, like a bird darting into a snare, little knowing it will cost him his life. Proverbs 7:22, 23

SINGAPORE BECKONED like the Emerald City. Its ultra-modern high-rise buildings appeared to grow out of the water and reach for the sky. The anchorage, where the America settled, was occupied by hundreds of ships. When liberty call was announced, Adam Price and I boarded a ferryboat for the twenty-minute ride into the city. The equatorial sun burnt our faces and arms.

Fleet landing was at a small shopping center with several camera stores and a money exchange. Dressed in tropical whites, shore patrol and New Zealand MPs stood about conversing with each other. The city was large enough that we could go anywhere without seeing other sailors from the America.

Orchard Road offered one shopping mall after another, each bigger than the last. Occasional downpours of rain gave temporary relief from the heat, but afterwards the air felt like a giant steam bath. The futuristic skyscrapers stood in contrast to the old Buddhist temples of Chinatown. Because of strict sanitation laws, there was not a scrap of paper or a cigarette butt on the ground. Even chewing gum was illegal.

After an extensive tour of the island on the second day, I had a taxi driver take me to a massage parlor. On a secluded street lined with quiet apartments the cab stopped in front of a one-story building with a large tinted window. A man came out and opened the cab door for me. Inside a lobby area were several young Chinese ladies watching a black-and-white television. They all looked to be in their late teens or early twenties. Most of them wore T-shirts and gym shorts, while a few wore tightly wrapped silk dresses. They all stared at me. I followed the man into a darkened hallway with red-papered walls.

"Wait here, please," said the man as he went into another room.

A minute later an older man came in, greeted me, and got to the point. "Massage and sex, seventy-five dollars."

He took my money then went out into the lobby and brought back a girl who looked about twenty. "This is Helen."

"Helen" led me into a bedroom with a round bed, ceiling mirrors, and more red wallpaper. This time I was neither nervous nor bothered by guilt. About twenty minutes later I left the room. Helen hardly looked at me the whole time and only said a few words in Chinese. I didn't want to leave her. It seemed like there should be something more. I thought it'd be nice to take her out to dinner, but she was a slave to pimps, and I meant nothing to her.

Back at my rack, I didn't pray for forgiveness, because I felt no guilt. *Maybe God realizes this is how it has to be for me. He has no wife for me, so apparently this is an acceptable alternative to Him.* I kept trying to fool myself.

After quarters, most of us were sent to the yellow gear storage area above the bomb farm to chip paint off a bulkhead. For over a month the chief had been thinking up work for us to do. Now that we were in port, he wanted us to repaint the skid stow. The heat was suffocating, and our dungarees were soaked with sweat. Only AO3 Brock Bowers, who was supervising, remained dry. The guy looked like a Ken doll, but had the emotional maturity of a twelve year old. Bowers did as little as possible and whined like an infant every time Crawford gave him an order. Because of constant grooming, his uniforms were always pressed and his boots shined like glass.

"You all look kinda hot," he said. "My goodness, you boys would never make it in Louisiana. None of you are going anywhere 'till this here bulkhead is chipped clean."

After a couple of hours we were dismissed. I got cleaned up and went out with Lee Fuller and Paul Whorely. Later that afternoon we entered a hotel cocktail lounge near fleet landing. Fuller left with some friends while Whorley and I drank Tiger Beer. Whorley said he needed to go back to the ship for more money.

"I don't know if I'd leave just yet," I said.

"How come?"

"Take a look."

A large number of shore patrol had gathered at fleet landing, and a lieutenant holding a portable radio was giving them instructions. Whoreley said it would be all right and left to get on a ferry returning to the ship. The other sailors were getting nervous. I decided to leave while I had the chance. Walking down a sidewalk, I happened to look at an English newspaper. An American Marine lieutenant colonel had been kidnapped and killed in Lebanon.

I knew anyone returning to the ship would not be allowed off again, and it was just a matter of time until the shore patrol started rounding everyone up. Desperately I tried to think of something to do before the rest of my liberty was cancelled. Only one thing came to mind, and I jumped into the first available cab. The girl I had this time called herself "Jenny." Before getting started, I tried to talk with her. Since she spoke English, and looked like a college student, I asked her if she attended school. She looked at me like it was the dumbest question ever.

Back at fleet landing, a horde of sailors waited to get on the liberty boats. Shore patrol, with their black billy clubs, pointed the way for those still loitering around the shops. It was a short port visit. *Now I'll just tell God I'm sorry and everything will be okay*, I thought.

In the G-1 shop everyone was talking about their new tattoos. Castille had other things he wanted to talk about. "I was at this bar, and I had seven whores."

Everyone laughed at him. "Castille, you're full of s---," someone said.

"Like hell I am. Ask Richardson."

AO2 Richardson sat at the forklift desk playing solitaire. While keeping his eyes on the cards he said, "He's right."

Castille folded his arms and looked at each of us with a proud smirk on his face. "I told you guys I had seven of 'em."

• • •

Word spread throughout the ship that we were going to Lebanon. When the anchor lifted, G-1 was on the hangar deck moving ordnance. Rain cascaded like a waterfall down the open aircraft elevators. It was disheartening to be leaving Singapore so soon, but I figured if we were speeding off to Lebanon there would be no loitering in the IO. I figured wrong. Instead of returning to the Mediterranean, the battle group did circles off the southern coast of Iran for another thirty days. Before we could get out of Singapore Harbor, I was told it was my turn to go TAD (Temporarily Assigned Duty). I would be away from G-1 for three months.

The LPO assigned me to S-11, which was a division made up entirely of TAD personnel. S-11 functioned as caretakers for the chief petty officers. Most of the personnel were assigned as compartment cleaners while others worked in the CPO's mess and scullery. The man in charge of S-11 was Chief Henry Lussow, who treated his men with total contempt. The news circling around the division was that Lussow was indirectly responsible for the deadly fire on May 13. Apparently, the captain felt he would do less damage as a mess caterer than as a gas jockey. He hated me from the moment we met, and I was sent to work in the forward CPO berthing, which is where he resided. The other cleaner down there was an AOAN named Ricky Reed from F-14 squadron VF-33. He was another Texan from Lubbock.

At times Lussow was impossible to work for. The chiefs had all kinds of junk scattered about their berthing. Lussow would tell me it was gear adrift and I needed to move it. No matter where Reed and I stowed the stuff, Lussow would say, "Get it out of there. It's gear adrift."

Lussow's stupid head games were so infuriating it took every ounce of self-control not to break his jaw. One afternoon he said, "You can't keep that stuff in the fan room, Porter, it's gear adrift. Now get rid of it, on the double!"

I said to him, "Okay Chief, it's gear adrift. So where do you want me to stow it?"

"That's your problem. Deal with it."

"Whatever you say, Chief."

I found a large box and filled it with the paperbacks and board games that had been the cause of my dilemma. When Sponson-6 was opened for trash dumping, I took the box topside and threw it overboard.

Living in the ship's TAD berthing was almost as bad as working for Lussow. Thievery was rampant, and everyone shared his locker with a hundred cockroaches. Looking at hardcore magazines was my only means of escape from the tension.

On September 5 our ship entered the Suez Canal. We wouldn't miss the humidity of the Red Sea. I stood on the bow of the flight deck as the ship entered the Mediterranean, and I filled my lungs with the cool, refreshing air.

Three days later the ship made a port visit at Toulon, France. It was the crew's first liberty since Singapore. While the rest of the crew were ashore, Lussow kept the S-11 members on the mess deck and in the berthing spaces until nearly 3:00 P.M. When I was finally allowed to go, I went ashore with Reed.

Toulon was an old city where a large French naval base was located. A stone castle overlooked the harbor. On the waterfront was an old sailing ship from the days of Napoleon. But the only thing on my mind was finding a prostitute. Close to fleet landing was a seedy walking street called "The Gut." Bars with loud music and scantily-dressed champagne girls, and pornographic video stores lined both sides of the street.

We entered one bar and heard Petty Officer Stewart yell, "Hey Porter, don't waste your time with these 'buy-me-drink' girls. They won't put out for nothin'. We've already tried and we're getting nowhere." Stewart was another guy who was married.

When it grew dark, Reed and I figured we might have better luck by asking a cab driver. The taxi took us away from the waterfront and eventually parked in front of a drab apartment building on a quiet street. The driver said something in French and pointed at the building. After charging us a double fare, he left us alone in that unknown part of the city.

Reed was tall and blond and wore cowboy boots and a huge rodeo buckle. He stood on the sidewalk looking around, and I could tell he was thinking the same thoughts I was thinking about the cab driver. "Where is this place?"

"I don't know. He was pointing at that building, but it's just apartments."

As we walked toward the building, Reed's boots clopped like horse hoofs against the concrete. The inside of the lobby consisted of dirty gray walls and a single bare light bulb hanging from the ceiling. We didn't know which apartment to go to. I knocked on a door and an intoxicated old man answered. He didn't speak any English, but he knew what we were after. This is how desperate I had become; knocking on the doors of strangers, hoping someone who looked the part would answer. The drunk flashed us a toothless smile and extended his hand for money. We gave him a few francs, and he pointed towards a door down the hall.

The man watched us walk to the other door. We knocked and a woman's voice asked, "Who est il?"

"Can we come in?" I asked in reply.

The woman began shouting at us from the other side of the door. Her angry monologue never allowed us to say another word and it was so loud the other tenants came out to see what was happening. The drunken man explained to everyone why we were there, and they all laughed. I felt myself flushing with humiliation.

"Vous etes la police. Part et me partir seul," said the woman's voice.

"No, we're not the police. Just let us in," I begged.

"Part et me partir seul," she repeated.

I looked at Reed, but he wasn't offering any help, and we had attracted quite a crowd by now. "Come on let's get out of here."

We quickly exited the lobby while the woman kept yelling.

Lost and frightened, I thought about my actions. Besides putting my safety at risk, I had been cheated out of my money and embarrassed, all because I was looking for a sexual encounter. I was not even in the mood for it, but something was driving me to accomplish this unholy quest. For some reason, I felt I could not enjoy the port visit until I engaged in intercourse. After several minutes, we found a taxi that returned us to fleet landing.

On our last day in Toulon, I was alone. I went into an adult bookstore and watched a pornographic video in a small booth. After that, I spent large amounts of money on the champagne girls, hoping one of them would take me to a private place. When my money ran out I returned to the exchange for more francs. At the far end of the Gut I found a bar with no other patrons inside. The female bartender offered to take me in a back room for forty-five dollars. She gave me only five minutes!

On the boat ride back to the ship I did not want to talk to anyone. I felt a gut-wrenching hatred toward myself. I did not even bother to ask God for forgiveness. Prayer was pointless; I was a degenerate beyond help. At least that's what I was thinking at the time. I could have gone to the chaplain's office for guidance and prayer from the staff of religious program specialists (RPs). However, I was too ashamed to admit my problem and I thought I was the only one with this condition. Oh sure, there were a lot of other guys doing the same thing, but I believed I was the only one addicted to it.

After boarding the ship I did have a brief laugh when I saw Petty Officer Bowers. One of the G-1 airmen, who had had enough of his bullying, saw him leave a café. The airman attacked him and wiped away his Ken doll looks. When I saw Bowers being helped to the infirmary, he looked like a character in a cartoon. He was minus a shoe, his clothes were shredded, and he had a black eye. Everyone who saw him limp by on the mess deck laughed out loud. It was a terrible thing to laugh at, but I was desperate for any kind of humor.

For two and a half weeks the battle group participated in naval exercises with the NATO allies. I had been moved out of the forward chiefs' berthing, and was made a compartment cleaner for the CPOs of HS-11, the air wing's helicopter squadron. The new job assignment was much easier. Since the air wing spaces were on the 03 level, Lussow was never around to check on me. Climbing those five ladders was just too much for him. Since several of the HS-11 chiefs worked nights, they did not want me in their berthing. In the morning, I would haul their dirty uniforms to the laundry compartment and return with them in the afternoon. In between those times I would take the trash out and do a quick sweep up. The rest of the time was spent with the other air-wing compartment cleaners in a supply closet reading paperbacks.

Since I did not have to work as hard during the day, I found it more difficult to sleep at night. Many of the guys in the berthing would play cards all night. The cockroaches scampered around looking for food. When I couldn't sleep, I'd fuel my addiction by looking at one of my sex magazines.

On October 11, the America arrived in the city-state of Monaco, the Beverly Hills of Europe. It was immediately apparent the place was far too expensive for an American sailor, so most of the crew took the train to Nice.

Nice was a beautiful city, but I inevitably ended up in the bad part of town. In a small working class bar, a Frenchman tried conversing with Reed and me in broken English.

"You are from the big American ship in Monte Carlo, yes?"

"We are," said Reed.

The Frenchman came over to the small table we were sitting at with drink in hand. He wore dirty jeans and matching jacket. "Is there something in particular you are looking for?" he asked in a quiet voice.

I didn't feel like talking to this dude, so I just sipped my drink while Reed answered. "Yeah, we're looking for some women. You know what kind we mean?"

The Frenchman laughed while taking a drink and some of the liquor splashed onto his jean-jacket. Reed hadn't said anything funny.

"Oui, I know what kind you mean. Wait here, maybe I can help."

He walked over to a woman at the bar, who was dressed like he was, and spoke to her. She looked over at us, said something to him, and continued sipping from her glass. The man returned to our table. "She will be happy to help you when she is through."

We knocked back several glasses of Scotch and hoped her looks would improve. They didn't. The woman took us back to her apartment. I waited outside while Reed went upstairs with her. When he was through, I went up. I felt the same way I had that night in Toulon; I didn't want to be there nor did I want to have sex with her. However, it was impossible for me to turn around and walk back down the stairs even though I was too drunk to perform. The inside of her apartment was filthy, and it stank as she did. I did what I had to do and got out.

The next morning, I felt dirty and I could still smell the stench of the woman. Jumping out of my rack onto some cockroaches, I threw my underwear into the TAD laundry (which was the same as throwing them into the trash, because nothing was ever returned) and climbed into the shower. I scrubbed and scrubbed, but felt as if I never would rid myself of the filth and stench. It was like Lady MacBeth trying to wash the blood stains from her hands.

The America left Monaco and returned to the western Mediterranean. The very next day it dropped anchor in Palma. It was at this last stop where I realized the extent of my problem. Reed and I ventured into Blood Alley, which was actually a maze of several alleys made up of drug dens, bars, and brothels. Many of the bars were showing pornographic videos, and every prostitute had two or more sailors trying to arrange a deal. The streets were covered with trash and broken beer bottles.

Reed pointed to a girl in a white sweater, surrounded by five guys from the ship. "I had that one last night, and she wasn't bad."

"What's her name?" I asked.

Reed thought for a minute. "Uh . . . Maria."

Maria was a pretty girl with wavy, shoulder-length brown hair. When our eyes met, she bolted from the group surrounding her and ran over to me. The jilted sailors began cursing her and one said to me, "Yo' man, that little 'ho is nothing but a b----."

They began walking towards us like they were going to hurt her, but one said, "Hell, we don't need to waste our time on that one. Let's go find another."

Maria stood behind me until they left. She then smiled at me, took my hand and led me to the brothel where she worked. At the top of a flight of narrow stairs sat a fat madam who took my money. We went into a room with only a small bed and a rusty sink. Afterwards, Maria escorted me outside while holding my hand. She kissed me goodbye. It was hard to leave her. Reed walked up to us, but she never acknowledged him.

"How was she?" he asked.

"You were right, she was great."

The following day I came back by myself looking for her. Because of the confusing layout of Blood Alley I could not find the exact location of where we had been the night before. Even in the middle of the day, a lot of sailors milled around looking for action. While speaking with an acquaintance from S-11, I felt someone put their arm around me and reach for my wallet. I turned and saw it was a homeless woman. She seemed to know why I was there, and begged me to take her. The woman was filthy; her skin and blonde hair were dark from dirt. Because it was early in the afternoon, there was not much of a selection. The woman repulsed me, she was far worse than the one in Nice; yet I agreed. The last thing I wanted was to have any physical contact with her, but I couldn't say no.

She insisted I pay her then and there, but I refused. She said I was to follow her, "Me siguen." She led me through

different alleys of the great maze, each one more sinister looking than the last. The further we walked, the fewer people
there were. Most of the doors had rusted padlocks. One alley
ended in a cul-de-sac surrounded by four small buildings that
had once been houses, but were abandoned years ago. We
stopped in front of one, which was missing its front, and
piles of rubble reached to the second floor. The neighborhood
looked like Berlin in 1945.

"Me dan el dinero ahora," the woman said with her hand
out.

"I'm not giving you any money. Where are we going?" I
asked nervously. I had no idea how to get out of there, and I
was beginning to seriously distrust the woman.

"Me dan el dinero. Primero, yo necesitan comprar cocaina,"
she said pointing to the house.

A large rat ran across the top of the rubble pile. "You're
going to get cocaine in there? Let's get out of here."

She was becoming more agitated and nervous as she stood
there thinking of what to do next. The drug addict and the
sex addict were both being tough with the negotiations. One
tried trickery and manipulation; the other tried to stand his
ground. Both wanted to exploit the other's weakness for their
personal gratification.

She led me back through the alleys. To my relief, I began
to see people again, and an occasional car. In front of a fairly
busy café she turned towards me and said, "Dinero, por favor.
Yo necesitan cocaina. I'll come back shortly."

This time I relented, since I just wanted to get this whole
thing over with. I handed her a wad of paper bills. She bolted
into the café. Immediately, I realized how foolish I had been
to give her the money. I ran inside the café and saw there was
a wide exit leading to a street. Outside of the exit I looked up
and down the street. She was gone. Who was I going to turn to
for help? The police? God?

Somehow, I found my way out of there and walked through the familiar area of shops and pubs near the cathedral. Inside Texas Jack's I had a bowl of chili and chastised myself for being so stupid. At that point, I only wanted to enjoy my food, have a couple of drinks, then return to the ship. This time I was not content with the experience of the night before, though, and felt I had to go back. I still had enough money.

Going back to Blood Alley was the last thing I wanted to do, but this demonic force would not relinquish its hold on me. I finished my lunch and returned to the maze of alleys behind the cathedral.

After a while, a prostitute stopped me and asked if I wanted to go upstairs. She was sitting outside a brothel, so I figured she was legitimate. I went inside with her. She took the last of my money, then got upset with me because I was not fast enough. After that I was flat broke. I didn't even have money for cab fare, so I had to walk three miles to fleet landing.

Back at the ship, Bowers was being helped across the mess deck to the infirmary. He looked like he had fallen asleep under a sunlamp and was on the verge of unconsciousness. Just like last time, everyone laughed. It turns out he had overdosed on some European tanning pills. He was lucky he didn't get written up; the pharmacies were off limits. When the laughing ended I went to the shower. I tried once more to rid myself of the filth. It seemed like nothing could cleanse the grime that was deep within me.

• • •

The America Battle Group was scheduled for military exercises off the Spanish coast before returning home. At this point, I was weary of the cruise and wanted to return to the states as much as the family men did. In the classified section of a hunting magazine, I saw an ad for guided hunts into the

Bob Marshall Wilderness of Montana. It didn't seem all that long ago I was in Montana dreaming about the far corners of the world. Now I was at one of those far corners, but I could only think about hunting in Montana. Although I denied it, I truly missed my relationship with Jesus. It had been shallow in times past, but now it was non-existent. I remembered attending New Life Christian Center with my family in Polson. Pastor Finch not only delivered thought-provoking sermons, but he perpetually emphasized the reverence Christians should have when entering the house of God. My reverence for the church extended only to standing when the pastor asked us to. I would not participate in worship, I did not close my eyes during prayer, and I usually read a book while the message was being delivered. My relationship with Christ was less than lukewarm. It was frozen.

How can I ever go back into that church and associate with those people? Maybe when I'm out of the Navy and away from the temptations, God will let me come back to Him.

Chief Lussow moved me back down to the third deck where Lee Fuller and I were responsible for the aft chiefs' berthing. Again, I was hauling laundry and scrubbing the deck from dawn to dusk.

The ship passed Gibraltar on November 1 and entered the Atlantic Ocean. The seas were much rougher than they had been in May, and gray clouds moved with the cold wind. It was not until the ship passed south of Bermuda that the waters calmed. As we approached the U.S., everyone became excited about the homecoming. Since all the chiefs lived off ship while in Norfolk, they packed their sea bags and threw away everything they did not want to take home. The berthing trash cans were overflowing, and Fuller and I spent hours just emptying them over the side.

In one trash can I found a videotape in perfect condition. *Why would anyone throw this away?* I wondered. There was no title or anything to indicate what was on the tape. A title was not necessary, though. I knew what I'd find on it and I kept it for myself. A year and a half later I would regret not having thrown it into the ocean.

On November 10 the America was moored again at Pier 11 in Norfolk. The pier was crowded with thousands of people holding balloons and *Welcome Home* signs. While wearing my dress blues, which now supported a single sea service ribbon, I looked at all those people and realized none of them were there for me. My family was on the other side of the continent. When I was finally allowed to leave, I went to an exchange post and had some pizza and beer for dinner. Then I went to the base library and read for a while. It was like any other day of liberty in Norfolk.

I never had to deal with Chief Lussow for the rest of the time I was TAD since he went on leave. While in Norfolk, I was assigned to clean a large chiefs' berthing on the 03 level. In the morning, a third class petty officer would check on me, then I would not see him the rest of the day. The berthing was a mess. For about a week, I filled up trash bags and carried them to the dumpsters at the street end of the pier. I found two perfectly good pairs of flight deck boots, so I threw away my boot camp boondockers. Any pornographic material I found, I kept.

Before I was able to finish hauling out the trash of the berthing, I was sent back to G-1. I was glad to be back and I never complained about the work there again. Chief Webb was a saint compared to Lussow. However, for the Christmas break I was sent back to S-11 to work in its scullery. I spent Christmas day with a fever while scrubbing pots and pans.

On December 27 I flew to Montana for two weeks' leave. My parents wanted to hear about the cruise. I had to guard everything I said. One night I watched the videotape I had taken from the trash. As expected, it was hardcore pornography. I hid it in an old shoebox inside my bedroom closet, which my parents were using for storage. It contained items that had not been moved since I was in high school. I was certain nobody would ever find it.

5
1990

Do not lust in your heart after her beauty or let her captivate you with her eyes, for the prostitute reduces you to a loaf of bread, and the adulteress preys upon your very life. Proverbs 6:25, 26

ON A COLD EVENING in January, I sat in the food court of the Navy Exchange. Scott Straub walked by with a tray of food, so I called him over to my table. He sat down and asked, "What are you doing this week-end? Man, we've got three days off."

"I don't know. Nothing, I guess."

"Let's take a road trip. I got my truck from Ohio."

"Okay, where do we go? Atlantic City?"

"Why not New York?"

We had become friends toward the end of the cruise. In a small café in Toulon we had gotten to know each other. The café was hard to find, so there weren't any other crew members there. Scott's stocky frame, tattoo-covered arms, and thinning blond hair made him look older than his nineteen years.

The next day at work was the same in-port routine. Reveille sounded at 6:00 A.M., and quarters a half-hour later. As always, G-1 formed up in the aft section of the hangar bay. Lazily, we formed into two ranks with hands stuffed into the insulated pockets of our green, foul-weather jackets.

"G-One, attention!" ordered the LPO. "Listen up for roll call!"

Everyone hated coming to attention, especially in the winter. Hands reluctantly withdrew from the warm pockets, and thumbs were aligned along the seams of our trousers. A cold wind swept off the Elizabeth River into the hangar bay. After quarters, we sat or stood in the shop watching MTV until Chief Webb dismissed us. Scott and I discussed our upcoming road trip with Wil Diaz while the TV showed the same stale videos. Diaz was from the Cuban section of Miami and claimed he was the illegitimate son of Fidel Castro. He knew New York City well. With a wicked smile he said, "Whatever you do, don't go to Forty Second Street."

"That's where we're going."

We sped off in Scott's white Toyota truck and spent the night in Dover, Delaware, then crossed over into New Jersey the next morning. The farther north we went, the colder it got. After three hours of driving we saw New York City's skyline.

"Hey, see that green thing sticking out of the water?" I asked

"Yeah."

"That's the Statue of Liberty."

We rested a while in our over-priced motel room in Jersey City. After dark, we drove through the Holland Tunnel into Manhattan. Forty Second Street was easy to find, and Scott parked the truck on a block one street to the south.

We walked for several blocks down 42nd, which was a world of blatant immorality inhabited by roving perverts. There were "arcades" with stacks of glossy sex magazines and peep shows in the back, while heavy metal music blasted from speakers. Pornographic movie houses were everywhere, and there were theaters with marquis, which read "Live All-Male Sex Show." Pimps and drug dealers roamed the sidewalks like hungry wolves. Male prostitutes wearing cowboy hats leaned against street lamps trying to make eye contact with men who walked by.

Scott and I went into one of the movie houses. Inside, it was hard for my eyes to adjust. The darkness made the customers feel inconspicuous. Men, young and old, rich and poor, milled around lustfully looking over one another. My own lust was replaced with fear. The surrounding darkness bristled of evil, and more than ever I longed for the safety of home. After half an hour I could no longer stand it. "Let's get out of here."

We found that someone had broken into Scott's truck by breaking out a side window. During the drive back a freezing wind blew into the car. My face and hands grew numb while I tried to figure out what I had been looking for. Porno tapes were not hard to get. Why had I gone all the way to New York to visit a sleazy X-rated theater?

• • •

"All right, those of you who don't have duty can take off," said the LPO.

Scott and I dropped down the scuttle and headed for the berthing to change clothes. We would eat at a local fast food restaurant then find a place to park while we split a pint of bourbon; every day it was the same. During the times we felt sociable, we'd stop by the unofficial G-1 apartment on Ocean Avenue. The guys on the lease were Wil Diaz, Manuel Pena, and Kevin Kelleher, but Chris Soukup and Kevin Langkam were always there as well. While the beer and liquor flowed, everybody talked about home or some misadventure they'd had overseas.

One night, Scott and Joe (another G-1 member) were arrested in the parking lot across from Pier 11. Scott had left the truck's gas cap at a station, so Joe decided to acquire one from another car. Neither realized the base police were staking out the parking lot. Instead of taking them to the brig, the police turned them over to the ship's master-at-arms. Both were sent to captain's mast, where each was reduced to pay grade E-1 (Airman Recruit) and restricted to ship for forty-five days. In the meantime, the truck was mine.

On weeknights I rarely left the base. Going to one of the E-Clubs or to the library was the highlight of my evenings. When the weekends came around, I'd rent a motel room (at a place called the Admiralty) and barricade myself there for two days. On Sundays, I would mill around Military Circle, the main shopping center in Norfolk, and catch a movie. Going to church never entered my mind. The routine became tedious.

There were many nights when I felt especially lonely and longed for the company of a woman. I often wished I were back in Spain or Singapore where obtaining one was so easy. In Virginia, activities of that nature were illegal and the laws were enforced. But I began looking for some kind of action. Not even the fear of arrest could harness the urge that raged within me. Once a month I would visit the massage parlor in Virginia Beach. I wanted to go more often, but each visit cost me a hundred dollars.

Late one night I drove up and down Ocean Avenue like a nocturnal predator. The girls were out there. In tight dresses, high heels, and wigs they stood in the shadows of the brick housing projects. Broken glass and empty twelve-pack boxes littered dirt yards that once had grass. Cars would pull alongside the curb and flash their lights at the girls. Further from town the hookers were not always female. Independent drag queens kept their distance from territories claimed by the pimps. The scene disgusted me. Mostly I was disgusted with myself. I returned to my motel room alone.

• • •

In March the America set sail for the first time since returning from the Mediterranean. We weren't going far, just down to the Caribbean, then a short visit to Fort Lauderdale. Most of my free time was spent on the whaleboat sponson next to AWSEP. The waters of the Bermuda Triangle were rough, and the hull took a tremendous beating.

God spared my life one night. I spent over an hour on the sponson while standing against the rusty railing. Huge waves crashed against the hull just below my feet. At times the waves peaked over the flight deck. I stepped through the open door of AWSEP to warm up. A few seconds after entering the shop a giant wave smashed into the sponson and seawater poured through the doorway covering the shop's deck. AO2 "Louie" Lewis swore out loud as everyone climbed the angles.

"Next time, Porter, close the damn door when you come in here," roared Lewis.

"You're the ones who had it open." I was drying my boots off with a rag.

An airman said to me, "You're lucky you came in when you did."

Out on the sponson, water was dripping from the whaleboat, the bulkheads, and the overhead. If I had stayed out there any longer, I would have been swept out to sea or crushed to death. I wondered why God had spared me when I was deserving of death.

•   •   •

When Scott completed his restriction to ship he was sentenced to three days of bread and water in the Norfolk Brig.

"Get me to Pizza Hut," he said while opening the passenger door of the truck upon his release.

Those three days must have been havoc for him. He ate a large pizza by himself. Then we drove all night to Ohio.

We visited his mother and friends, and I was introduced to White Castle hamburgers. Not all of our activities were so innocent. While driving through the side streets of Columbus one night we found an adult bookstore. There were no windows, and the only lighting was from a single bulb above the door. Inside, an intoxicated woman wearing only the bottom part of a bikini, was talking to the cashier. In the back, were several video booths offered a choice of ten different films to watch.

There were several men in the booth area; all wore gym clothes for easy removal. One man did nothing but walk up and down the aisle peering into each booth hoping to get invited inside. There were no doors on the booths, so the occupants were clearly visible. A couple of men masturbated to the videos in plain view of everyone. They were totally oblivious to their surroundings and acted out of compulsion. *Is this what I'm going to become?* I thought. *Or am I already there? … Why am I here, anyway?*

For two days in April I attended the Damage Control Petty Officer School in Norfolk while the ship began a major overhaul at the Portsmouth shipyard. The transfer to the DC work center allowed me to work independently without supervision. Even though I was doing a petty officer's job, I was still an airman.

It was a long hot summer. Practically every square inch of steel had to be sanded, painted, or welded. The heat made everyone sluggish and made the work that much harder. At night I couldn't sleep since the air conditioning units were being renovated. It was like being back on the equator, except we had liberty. The work intensified in July.

During a scorching afternoon I decided to pay a visit to the massage parlor. The woman I was with called herself "Betty." While we were getting dressed she said, "Come back next week."

"Next week? No way, I can't afford that. I'll come back next month when I have more money."

"No, no, I can't do it next month, I'll be somewhere else."

"Where are you going?"

"I don't know," Betty answered. "Where ever the owners send us. Every month they move us to another place. Last month I was in some other state."

There was sadness in her voice, and I didn't know what to say. We said goodbye and I walked away. It bothered me to be patronizing an Asian prostitution ring, but my lust overrode any sense of decency.

One night after a small G-1 party at the Ocean Avenue apartment, I stood by Scott's truck waiting for him. A block away, a couple of black girls, painted up and wearing tight-fitting clothes in bright colors, were talking. A small car pulled over to the curb where they stood, and turned out its lights. The white girls didn't advertise. They only came out of hiding when spotting a potential john. A skinny blonde teen wearing gym shorts, a white T-shirt and sandals came up to me and asked, "You looking for a date? Uh, are you a cop?"

"Yes to your first question and no to your second," I said.

"Okay, give me fifty bucks now and I'll meet you at the hotel across the street in ten minutes."

"No chance."

Nervously she continued. "Well you see, you pay me the money now and I let you touch me here so I know you're not a cop, then we meet across the street."

"That doesn't make any sense. Forget it." The girl reminded me of the druggie who ripped me off in Palma. Meanwhile, a girl in faded jeans and sweatshirt started talking to Scott as he unlocked the truck. They headed toward a nearby house.

"Hey Jake, come on." Scott waved me over.

I told "Blondie" to get lost. When I went over to Scott the girl with him shook my hand and said, "Hi, I'm Dawn. Your name is Jake?"

"Yeah."

"You don't want to mess with that girl you were talking to; she'll just take your money and split."

Dawn was similar to "Blondie" in stature, but had brown hair and was a couple years older. Inside the house, Dawn led me to a back bedroom. Toys and dirty diapers littered the hall. A Mickey Mouse lamp without a shade lighted the bedroom. Scott sat on the couch with her black boyfriend and watched television. When it was his turn, I sat on the couch.

"Bet you feel like a new man," said the boyfriend, smiling.

"Oh, yeah," I forced myself to say while thinking, *How does this guy just sit here watching TV while his girlfriend is taking strangers into the bedroom?* The air smelled of marijuana and excrement. More dirty diapers lay under the couch.

The couple was impoverished and this was how they made extra money. As Scott and I were leaving, other sailors were knocking at the door.

• • •

The America slipped from its berth on August 2 with the aid of several tugboats. The dirty water of the yard was brown as chocolate and small white crabs briefly broke the surface. That afternoon the ship was back in the Atlantic for sea trials. In October it sailed down to the Caribbean and we filled the magazines with bombs. Our new chief told the division that we would probably be going to war in the Persian Gulf. When the on load was complete we had six days of liberty in the Virgin Islands.

I got two weeks leave in December, but I was called back on Christmas night. It was official. The threat of war was plausible, and the ship had to be in the Red Sea by January 15, 1991. On the morning of December 28 the pier was packed with the ship's crew. Some wore dress blues, some wore dungarees, and some wore civvies; all carried sea bags. Scott and I leaned against the gunwale on the right side of the ship's tower and looked at the scene below. The sky was gray and the wind made flags and pennants snap smartly on the yardarms.

"Are you ready for it?" asked Scott.

"Ready for what?"

"Ready for war." Scott tried to light a cigarette in the wind.

"We're not going to war. We'll get all the way out there and then somebody will chicken out. And you can bet the captain will take his time coming home," I said, looking at the crowd. Guys in pea coats and white caps kissed their wives goodbye. "Look at that. Man, there ain't nobody down there to see us off."

"Yeah, well what are you gonna do?" The cigarette dangled from Scott's lips.

"And there's not going to be anyone for us when we get back. Come on, it's cold up here; let's get below."

By noon, the mooring lines were cast off and we began the long voyage to the Middle East.

6
DESERT STORM

You have cut short the days of his youth; You have covered him with a mantle of shame. Psalm 89:45

THE AMERICA PLOUGHED EAST through the choppy waters of the Atlantic. I put on a red jersey, olive drab BDU trousers, and flight-deck boots—the only apparel I would wear for the next two and a half months. At 7:00 P.M. I climbed up into the main shop and headed for the division office to check my scheduled maintenance. While walking past some lockers I saw an airman named Patrick White.

The shop lockers looked as if they had been found in an urban ghetto. The flimsy metal cabinets were crisscrossed with different colors of spray paint. White was standing in front of his, reading a Christmas card. He was small in stature and had a shock of red hair that stood on end. The hangar deck supervisor worked him relentlessly. His dirty jersey and dungaree pants attested to the hardships he endured, yet he was quiet and never complained.

It was unusual for me to ask somebody about a personal letter, but I found myself standing next to him and reading the card. "Hey Whity, who sent you that?" I asked.

"I don't know," he mused, "some girl in the Philippines. I'm not even sure how she got my address."

"Are you going to write her back?"

"Uh, I don't know. I've already got a girlfriend."

I snatched the Christmas card from his fingers and copied down the return address. "Okay, then I'll write her."

Her name was Felicia and she wanted an American pen pal. If I didn't rush things or make assumptions, I felt maybe I could get myself a wife. With a wife I'd be free from my addiction—or so I thought.

The ship was a swarm of activity, but morale was high. There were no inspections or unnecessary work, because there were plenty of legitimate tasks for everyone. My supervisor, Greg Parker, and I made up the entire DC work center. The junior airman of our team had received a Bad Conduct Discharge for breaking into cars and was never replaced. Parker worked day check and I worked nights. I usually finished my work in two or three hours, and the rest of the night I'd spend watching movies with the office staff.

On New Years Eve the ship was halfway across the Atlantic. At midnight, several members from the hangar deck and forklift crew pulled out bottles of rum and vodka from their shop lockers. Two nights later, AO1 J. D. McKay, the night check supervisor, called me over to the LPO desk. McKay was a stocky New Yorker who lived on a steady diet of coffee and cigarettes. He was responsible for the TAD rotation, and in his green hardback notebook he showed me that my name was at the top of the list.

"I have to send you to the mess deck. We don't have anymore new people, and all of the other airmen have already had their turn. When we run out of new people we have to send the old ones back," he explained gravely.

I was devastated. We were sailing into history, and the only thing I'd be doing was slopping beans onto plastic trays. I appealed to Parker, but there was nothing he could do. The next day I reported to the ship's personnel office to start the TAD processing, which included a medical exam. I failed it with flying colors. Somehow, I contracted a severe case of scabies that covered me from the neck down. The doctor prescribed a bottle of medicated soap and said there was no way I was going to be working around food. It didn't get me out of TAD, but at least I wouldn't have to work on the mess deck.

Later in the evening I had to report back to the G-1 LPO to see where I was being sent. Parker stopped me in the shop. "Just go about your normal routine tonight. You're not going TAD." It was the best news I had received in a while.

Since I was the only airman who was DCPO certified, the division decided they couldn't afford to let me go for three months.

"I bet you think you're pretty slick going over my head," said McKay while sitting at the LPO desk.

I had merely been passing through the office to check my assignments. "What are you talking about?"

"You know what I'm talking about. When I told you that you were going TAD you went and complained," said McKay.

I had socialized with McKay during the various division barbeques, but now he was acting paranoid as if there were some conspiracy on my part to undermine his authority.

"I didn't have anything to say about it," I replied.

"Just be careful, I'll be watching you."

"All right McKay, you've got me scared."

On January 9 the ship passed through the Straits of Gibraltar. The Rock's peak rose above a thick layer of haze. HS-11 helos scouted the area and watched the merchant ships heading in the opposite direction. Four days later I composed a letter for Felicia. I tried to sound interested, but not desperate.

The America entered the Suez Canal at 3:00 A.M. on January 15. I recognized the putrid smell of decaying fish. It was much colder than before. A couple of hours later, the sun appeared as a giant orange semi-circle above the ancient dunes of the Sinai Desert. As it rose higher into the sky, the air warmed slightly. The UN deadline for Iraq's withdrawal from Kuwait had been reached, and nothing in the Middle East had changed.

For most of the day, Scott and I stood on the flight deck. GMs behind .50 caliber machine guns were placed at various locations on the catwalk. Along the canal, peasants—dressed in filthy robes and turbans—waved to the crew members. For those standing at a distance, the ship appeared to be a steel behemoth stranded amongst the sand dunes.

As the ship entered the Red Sea, the sun began to set behind the mosque at El Suweis. I watched the silhouetted twin towers topped with small crescent moons for as long as I could and wondered what was going to happen now that we were on station.

The carriers Saratoga and John F. Kennedy were already there waiting for us. For the next month, the air wings of two carriers would attack targets in Iraq while the other flew air patrol over the task force. Each night I'd help move ordnance on deck then perform my scheduled maintenance. The days turned to weeks and the war became routine. While the planes were carrying out their missions there was a lot of down time. I used the time to pursue my obsession. Every unit within the war zone received mail sacks full of letters addressed to "Any Serviceman." A division on the ship could take as much as they wanted. Women looking for companions wrote most of the letters, so I jumped at the opportunity. I responded to several and got replies from most them. My choices were soon narrowed to Kim in San Leandro, California, and Jennifer in Scranton, Pennsylvania.

• • •

After much anticipation, I finally received a letter from the Philippines. Felicia said she was happy to receive my letter and was interested in corresponding with me. Over and over I read her letter until I had it memorized. I was totally smitten. I still stayed in contact with Kim and Jennifer as insurance. All three of them were asking for my picture. The most recent pictures of me were the ones taken during boot camp. In the pictures I was sickly and had a bad haircut. I wrote my parents, explained the situation, and asked if they'd send me some copies of my senior picture from high school.

On February 13, the America turned south en route for the Persian Gulf where it would provide air support for the upcoming ground offensive. During a lull in the air campaign, the ship had a change of command for a new captain.

Around this time I received a letter from my dad in regards to the pictures I'd asked for. He told me he'd been unable to locate the photos I wanted, but while searching my closet he found a videotape. I knew right away it was that porno tape I had found during the Med Cruise. He apologized for throwing it away. I could almost see the disappointed look on his face as he played the tape in his VCR. My euphoria for the war shattered in a second. The letters of support from relatives and friends, saying how proud they were of me, no longer mattered. My father had gotten a glimpse of my secret world and my immoral and perverted self was exposed.

• • •

While cruising through the Gulf of Aden, the crew was allowed to stand down. On our forty-fifth day at sea everyone was allotted two cans of Heineken during a steel beach picnic on the flight deck.

Wil and I would have mid-rats (mid-night rations) together on the mess deck, which G-3 was using as its own bomb farm. (The bombs, that took every bit of deck space in the crew's lounge, were fused and ready for delivery.) The food was usually so bad I'd stick to the chili bar. When the chili started being made with Polish sausage and spaghetti noodles, it became inedible as well.

Then, instead of mid-rats, I ate venison jerky and honey roasted peanuts sent to me from home and M&Ms donated to the ship by the Mars Company. I must have eaten more M&Ms on that cruise than I had throughout my entire life. Since the ship was south of the fighting, it became much hotter, and sodas were precious commodities. The ship's gedunk stores sold cans of 7-Up, Coke, and Pepsi with Arabic labels. The sodas were warm and flat.

Five days after leaving the Red Sea, the ship passed through the Straits of Hormuz and joined the Persian Gulf Battle Force. One morning the ship almost struck a mine. I was depressed again and getting blown to bits by a mine didn't seem that bad of a possibility.

When the war ended I'd go back to being a nobody indulging in his addiction. I had prayed for forgiveness dozens of times, but I didn't feel any different, and God seemed far away. Given the chance, I'd commit the same sins all over again. I wished God would just allow me to die. I paid a visit to the EOD (Explosive Ordnance Disposal) team hoping for a more dangerous job. EOD evolved from the frogmen of World War II, and they specialized in blowing up mines and other obstacles. However, their training lasted up to a year and I would've had to extend my enlistment. The war would be over in a few weeks, so I didn't follow through.

My father's letter still haunted me, and the ones I sent home became less frequent. I was ashamed and angry that he had discovered my secret life. When a local bank officer told my dad that my payments on a loan were coming in late, he sent me a letter explaining the problem. My sick mind construed the notion he and the bank officer, who didn't even know me, were trying to add to my daily stress. I fired off a response telling him I had enough to worry about. This war was my reality, and Polson, Montana was only a memory. Paranoia gripped me. My secret life was causing me to break down mentally.

•   •   •

Most of us were proud to be contributing our small piece of history, but now the cruise was in its sixth week and I was tired of it. The only time I helped in moving ordnance was when ordered to. After twelve hours of work I couldn't get to sleep. Most of my off duty hours were spent borrowing CDs and recording them on to blank cassettes. Several times I stayed up until noon and had lunch with Jim Wells. Jim was from Georgia and when he spoke of the church youth group he used to attend it sounded very much like the ones I had been a part of.

"I was going to church and youth group on a regular basis," said Jim, sitting on the edge of his rack. "But then something happened. I'm not sure why; I just stopped going."

Jim was short and stocky with brown hair. He'd been an aid in the Weapons Office the day I reported on board. Back then he got to sit in a comfortable chair while wearing starched dungarees, but now he was moving those big firecrackers around with the rest of us. During a previous discussion he told me his father was in prison, so maybe that was his reason for no longer going to church.

"I used to go to church also," I said.

Jim looked up at me. "You did?"

I told him about the churches, youth groups, and Christian schools I had attended.

"Do you go to the ship's chapel services?" he asked.

I stared at the dog tag laced to my left boot. "No. I can't bring myself to go in there. I went to chapel once at A-school, but I haven't been back since."

On February 28, a cease-fire was declared. When the

admiral announced the war's end over the 1MC, nobody cheered. There was never any doubt how it would end, but everyone was glad to be going home. Over the flight deck's public address system, Lee Greenwood's "God Bless the USA" played as the USS Theodore Roosevelt sailed off the port side.

Two weeks later, after seventy-eight consecutive days at sea, the ship dropped anchor at Hurghada, Egypt. For the first time in 1991, I put on civilian clothes and set foot on dry land. Over the next few days I traveled the country that had been the land of bondage for the Israelites. My life was in its own land of bondage. For several months the addiction had been dormant, but I knew it was still there. It lay just beneath the surface, waiting for an opportunity to erupt. I hated being a slave and wondered, *Where is my deliverer?*

7
TROUBLE IN NEW YORK

*Your wickedness will punish you; your backsliding will rebuke you.
Consider then and realize how evil and bitter it is for you when
you forsake the Lord your God and have no awe of Me, declares the
Lord, the Lord Almighty.* Jeremiah 2:19

I THOUGHT ABOUT FELICIA all the time. Now that I was back
in the USA, her letters arrived more frequently. She sent me
pictures of herself, which I looked at every chance I got. I
didn't think of her the same way as the other two women I
was writing to. Even though I hadn't met her yet, she was
someone special to me. Every time I wrote her a letter I was
very careful what I said.

The America did not remain at Pier-11 for long. It moved
up river to the shipyard in Portsmouth. It was scheduled for a
minor retrofit, and I hoped we weren't going to spend another
scorching summer in the yards without air conditioning. I was
checking my maintenance for the week when McKay called
me over to the LPO desk.

"What's up?" I asked.

"You're goin' TAD tomorrow and this time you're not
going to weasel out of it." McKay looked up at me.

"I didn't weasel out of it the last time."

"Tomorrow you start fire watch, and no one's gonna save
you this time."

I was upset, not with having to go TAD, but with the way he told me. McKay would fraternize with airmen one day, then drop his three chevrons on them the next.

This time around, the TAD wasn't so bad, and if McKay realized how easy I had it he never would have sent me. Each duty section of the fire watch division worked twenty-four hours then had forty-eight off. The ship was scheduled to take part in New York City's fleet week and Desert Storm Victory Parade in June. Sections of the ship needed to be repaired, and every space repainted. Civilian welders were hired to do hundreds of spot jobs, and I'd be assigned to one to make sure he/she didn't accidentally start a fire.

• • •

Writing letters to three different women had been exciting back in February, but now I was only thinking of Felicia and writing to her regularly. She was on the other side of the world, though, and I still had a year and a half left of my enlistment.

A few blocks south of the main gate at the Norfolk base was a dive called "Diamond Lil's." The place offered two brands of beer and a greasy grill. On the wall behind the bar were blue ball caps from every ship in the Tidewater Area. It was there I met Hue. She was a Vietnamese girl about twenty years old. Hue was a bartender there, and during the slow afternoon hours she would spend much of the time visiting with me. I wasn't even bothered that she was a Buddhist.

After a couple of weeks, it became clear she was taking advantage of me. Every day she wanted me to buy her lunch, or go to the grocery store to get her something. Whenever we were supposed to meet for a date, she failed to arrive. She turned out to be like those champagne girls in Europe. On another occasion, I overheard a different bartender and a regular barfly talking about Hue. The two women disliked her because of the way she manipulated lonely-hearted sailors. I was sick of the charade and wondered why it was so hard to find a genuine relationship.

· · ·

The weather turned warm in April. I sat on the whaleboat sponson and looked at the calm brown river. It was the twenty-ninth and something was troubling me. It would have been my sister's twenty-first birthday had she lived. Without warning, I sobbed and tears streamed down my cheeks. I couldn't understand what was wrong with me, since it had happened so long ago. Why was I so disturbed over a baby who died twenty-one years ago? I forced myself to think of something else and regained my composure. Anybody could have walked out there.

Two weeks later I was cutting through the G-1 shop on my way to evening chow. Meals were the only breaks I got while on fire watch. Greg Parker sat at the DCPO desk and when he saw me he asked, "Hey Jake, have you seen Gunner yet?"

"No," I said cautiously. I never liked it when officers were looking for me.

"He's got a Red Cross message for you. Go see him at the quarter deck."

A message from the Red Cross was always bad news. Gunner Weaver was acting as OOD at the quarterdeck. I approached the wooden lectern and saluted him. "You wished to see me, Sir?"

Gunner returned my salute. "Uh, yes I did, Porter." He looked over the message again before telling me what it said. "I hate to have to be the one to tell you this, but your grandfather has died. Your . . . uh . . . father wanted you to know."

I thanked him for telling me, then went to chow.

There wasn't any problem getting my leave approved. G-1 sent a replacement to the fire watch division, and I soon boarded a plane to California. Many friends and relatives attended the memorial service. I hadn't realized how much time had passed since seeing my brother, Keith. He had been with Youth With A Mission for two years at the Montana base in Lakeside and had let his hair grow long. Some of his friends and he had formed a Christian rock band that ministered to teenagers. Keith had chosen a different path in life, and I was envious that he'd been able to reject temptation. He was a willing servant of Christ, while I was an involuntary slave to Satan. The day after the memorial service, I drove to Montana with my dad and Keith while my mother remained behind with her mom.

Even though it was May, the weather in Montana was cool and overcast. With my mother still in California, my brother at the YWAM base, and my dad working all day, I quickly grew bored. During the afternoon and at night I'd often slip into one of the bars on Main Street. Even when my dad was home I felt awkward, because I had so much to hide. He was proud of my service in the Gulf War, but I knew my veteran status was superficial. The war would have been won even if I had stayed home. My personal "achievements" were made in seedy bars and dingy brothels around the world.

On Sunday I wore my tropical whites to church. Everyone came up to me after the service and welcomed me home like I was someone important. In front of them I tried to act like the clean-cut Christian boy who was serving his country, but I was a phony. Back at the house, I grew more restless and I missed my Navy buddies and our carousing.

When I returned to the ship it was still in Portsmouth. After only a couple of weeks back at fire watch, the division was decommissioned, and I returned to G-1. Now that it had a new makeover, the ship began its short voyage up the coast to New York. AO1 DeLey stopped me in the hangar bay. "Hey Porter, congratulations."

I returned his handshake and asked, "For what?"

"Crawford called last night and told me you made third."

"Really? I made third?"

"Yeah, but it's not official until July fifteenth."

I had finally been promoted to petty officer.

On June 6 the America arrived at New York Harbor, which was full of American and British ships. After changing into dress whites, liberty boats took us to Staten Island where we could catch the ferry into Manhattan. Scott had duty the first day, so I went ashore with Eddie Carrillo. Eddie was a local street-smart hustler. Over time we became friends, even though I didn't like him much. Prior to joining the Navy, I had been a criminal justice student and he had been a drug dealer.

"Other guys would get caught, because they looked liked s---," he once told me. "Long hair, beards, raggedy-ass clothes, but not me. I always had a haircut and a shave and wore new running suits. Carried the goods in a new gym bag and would wave to the cops when they drove by."

On the Staten Island Ferry we sat amongst the sailors and local commuters. Two young recruits were talking about where they wanted to visit. One said, "The first place I'm going to is Forty-Second Street."

Sitting across from them was a big Italian guy who looked like a leg breaker for some Jersey loan shark. With a huge cigar stuck between his fat fingers, he leaned forward and said to them, "You twos stay away from Forty-Second Street, you hear me? There ain't nothing there that's good for you."

The two young airmen hadn't been out of boot camp for very long, but they were already hooked to the seedier side of liberty. Carrillo and I both heard the advice and laughed to ourselves.

"Stick with me Porter and you won't need to go to Forty-Second, either," said Carrillo.

I didn't say anything.

"You always pay for it, don't you? How come?" asked Carrillo.

"I guess I'm just not as lucky as you," I answered. "Besides, while you're still trying to seduce some gal for hours at a time, I'm done and on my way."

"Well, I may strike out a lot, but every once in a while I'll hit a homer. Stick with me, Porter, and I'll show you the town. I know this city like the back of my hand."

We spent the rest of the day roaming the streets of lower Manhattan and somewhere along the way two strays from the division invited themselves along. One of these unwelcome guests was Pete Castile who had bragged about being with seven women during a single night in Singapore. He was now a petty officer, which according to regulations, put him in charge. I never could stand him or that Airman Recruit Clay he brought with him. Castile was arrogant and proud of his deviant behavior. Clay was a Black Muslim with a lot of beliefs that rubbed me the wrong way. It's unclear how those two ended up as liberty buddies.

"Hey Eddie, let's go to Little Italy and see some mobsters," I joked.

Carrillo thought for a moment. "Okay, let's go."

All four of us got into a cab and went to Canal Street. We walked into a bar lined with dark wood paneling. Sitting at a small table in the corner were a couple of goons right out of The Godfather. They had it all—dark silk suits, diamond rings, fat cigars—and they raised their glasses to us as we walked by.

"What'll it be gentlemen?" asked the bartender as we sat on the black padded stools.

We named our poison and Clay had orange juice. After the drinks were poured, Carrillo and the bartender began talking as if they had known each other for years. The owner and his son came out and joined in the conversation.

"How long have you owned the place?" Carrillo asked.

"A long time," said the owner. "My father owned it before me and my grandfather before him. Over in that spot there, I ran right into Bugsy Siegel and spilt his drink when I was a kid. My grandfather could have killed me."

Carrillo changed the subject. "Hey, where can we find some women around here?"

Castile was all ears.

"I don't know about that kind of stuff. You better talk to my son here," said the owner.

The conversation gradually became more coarse and loud. Carrillo could talk like a car salesman and lie just as well. Clay and I sipped our drinks while the others told their stories. Trouble began when a blonde woman walked in and sat at one end of the bar.

The bartender excused himself and walked over to where she sat. After fixing her a screwdriver he came back and refilled our glasses. "This round's on Millie," he said.

We raised our glasses to the lady and said thanks.

"You're welcome," she said.

This time the owner changed the topic. "So, were you guys over in the Persian Gulf?"

Carrillo shifted gears without hesitation and began telling sea stories. He sounded like the greatest seafarer since Horatio Nelson. Meanwhile, Castile got up with his drink and sat next to Millie. I don't know how to measure degrees of an addiction or whether Castile had it worse than I, but I was certainly more tactful. Pornography had distorted my perception of promiscuous women, but Castile seemed to be lacking all common sense. It's one thing to talk like a sailor when at sea, but when in port, one has to make adjustments when mingling with civilians. He was talking to Millie as if she were some down-and-out hooker on skid row.

Our three hosts weren't listening to Carrillo, because they

were watching what was transpiring at the far end of the bar. The lady had only intended to buy four Desert Storm Veterans a drink, and Castile thought she was making a play for him.

Millie slammed her glass down and said, "I have never heard such filthy talk in my life."

"What do you mean, you're a school teacher aren't you?" said Castile.

The owner went over to where they sat and asked, "What's the trouble here?"

Millie repeated what he had said. Carrillo never noticed what was happening and kept on rambling. The owner came back to us and said, "All right, time to settle up."

The two goons in the back, who had never said a word, stood up and buttoned their suit jackets, staring at us. I was 6 feet and 200 pounds, but those guys practically filled the room by themselves. We put our money on the bar, and I said to Carrillo, "Let's get out of here."

"What for? Let's get another round."

"He's right, man. Let's split," said Clay who also smelt trouble.

Reluctantly, Carrillo got off his stool and followed me to the door. Castile didn't have a clue and was still making sexual suggestions to Millie. I was going to leave him, but Carrillo said, "Come on Pete, we're going."

"What for?" asked Castile. "We just got here."

"I don't know, something's up."

Outside on the sidewalk Castile said, "What's the matter with you guys? I was this close to going home with that broad."

Carrillo turned to me and said, "What's up Porter, why'd you drag us out of there?"

"Open your eyes, dude," I said, and then pointed at Castile. "This guy got us kicked out of there and if we hadn't left they would've thrown us through the windows."

Carrillo was finally catching on. "What did you say to that lady in there?"

Castile repeated what he had said.

"What in the hell is the matter with you?" shouted Carrillo, poking Castile in the chest. "You don't go walking into a joint run by wise guys and start talking to a lady like that. Don't let it happen again!"

Later that evening we ended up in a club on East 42nd Street that was filled with rich young singles. We were asked to leave the place after Castile got in a shoving match with a jealous boyfriend. I was fed up and set off for Grand Central Station on my own.

The day after the victory parade the America sailed out of the harbor with little fanfare. Scott Straub and I hadn't been able to go ashore together, so we visited on the flight deck while I took pictures of the Statue of Liberty, the World Trade Center, the Empire State Building, and Ellis Island.

Back in Norfolk everyone returned to the same liberty routine. Every night we met at the apartment, did some heavy drinking, and then maybe went cruising for a little "action." I was sick of it and hated what I was becoming. AA Justin Sprague, who was a regular at the apartment, told me he'd met a lady who worked out of her home. He'd been with her a few times, and she was always available. One afternoon he invited me to come along with him to her house. Even though I wanted to, I was putting myself through the white-knuckle cure.

"No, I better not. Thanks anyway."

"What's the matter, are you getting morals now?" he demanded.

"Maybe I am," I answered. "I just don't want to be doing that anymore."

Sprague went to the woman's house alone.

In July my promotion was official and I got to put the

chevron and crow onto all my uniforms. Two months later, I had to say good-bye to two of my closest friends. Manuel Pena was returning to New Mexico and Scott was going back to Ohio. They had spent three years on active duty and would spend another three years in the reserves. Most of the guys who had been in G-1 when I arrived were gone now. Wil Diaz was one of the few still remaining who had arrived the same time as I. He had also been promoted to third class.

Letters from Kim and Jennifer became scarce and eventually stopped. Felicia and I were writing each other three or four times a week. Our letters became more personal, and we kept exchanging photos of ourselves. The G-1 LPO took me to the legal department, so I could inquire about bringing her into the country. The legal officer politely told me there was no chance unless we were already married.

In mid September the ship crossed the North Atlantic for a NATO exercise in the Vest Fjord of Norway. After a month in the frigid waters we were given six days of liberty at Portsmouth, England. Carrillo and I took in London and Stonehenge without any embarrassing episodes. Castile came up to me in the shop on my duty day and asked, "Hey, have you found a whorehouse yet?"

My temper was at the brink. *What do you care? I hate your guts*, my mind screamed. "No," I said.

He started writing on a piece of paper and said, "I found a good one by the beach. Here's the address. Just push the button on the voice box and . . ."

"I don't go to those places anymore," I interrupted.

"What do mean?" he looked confused.

"I mean it's over for me."

Letters from Felicia were arriving frequently, and I started to feel my addiction was cured. However, just as the waters seemed calm, a hurricane came my way.

While the ship was moored in Norfolk on a cool November

morning, I sat at the DC desk waiting for the chief to dismiss us. Mail call had been announced, and everyone was sitting around the shop reading their letters from home. I had received another airmail envelope from the Philippines and anxiously tore it open. The news inside hit me like a fist.

Felicia told me a co-worker had forced himself upon her the previous summer and she was about to give birth. She further explained that she understood my disappointment in her and she would no longer bother me with any more letters. I was suddenly confused and hurt. Mostly, I was angry with God.

When I was able to compose myself, I wrote back begging her not to stop writing to me. Since I was no longer in contact with Kim and Jennifer, I was right back where I started. Once again, I hit rock bottom. I envisioned God sitting in Heaven and having a good laugh as He led me from one disappointment to another. I walked to the E-Club and knocked back one whiskey and Coke after another. A sailor from another ship saw me and could tell something was wrong. He bought me a drink and told me not to do anything rash. Back on the ship, I found a place where I could be alone and cried out an angry prayer to God.

"How could You hurt me this way?" I demanded. "I can't believe You'd let somebody get raped in order to punish me. I keep trying to find a girl to marry, but You keep getting in the way or taking her from me. No more. If I have to go back to prostitutes, then I will!"

8
GOOD LONG ENOUGH

Resentment kills a fool, and envy slays the simple. Job 5:2

ON DECEMBER 4 the America left Norfolk and set sail on its third cruise of the year. Just before getting underway, I received a letter from Felicia telling me she had given birth to a girl and named her Sophia. She was grateful I had forgiven her and was happy I wanted to continue writing. I told her she had done nothing that required forgiving from me. However, I was still angry with God for allowing Felicia to be violated. Felicia and I were back to corresponding, but I was still determined to do whatever I wanted.

Right from the start, I could tell this Med Cruise was going to be as agonizing as my first. The division received two new CPOs, as if one wasn't enough. Chiefs Beavins and Huffington were a salt and pepper team that created a reign of terror the moment they arrived. Behind their backs they were called the "Dastardly Duo." They gave EMI and threatened captain's mast for the slightest infractions. Even first-class petty officers with sixteen years experience were not exempt from their bullying. Gunner Weaver had transferred to the new super carrier USS George Washington, and the new division officer was the same age as I. He was a spineless leader who never seemed to be around. The chiefs operated with absolute impunity. The new gun-boss was an arrogant pilot named

Commander Edison who was an opportunist that followed the XO around like a lost puppy. Self-aggrandizing ticket punchers held every link in the chain of command.

Parker was moved to forklifts, and AO1 Bob Schofield and AO2 Ernie Schwartz, who were transferred from shore duty billets, moved into DC. The chiefs forbade them to sign off any maintenance. All the assignments to our work center had to be performed and signed off by me. DC was the only work center in G-1 where there were more supervisors than workers. The division was top heavy.

A rift evolved between those of us who had been in the war and those who had not. At this point, all of the veterans in G-1 were petty officers or senior airmen. We were wedged between green recruits who were in high school during the war and three khakis that watched it on CNN. The chiefs tried to break us at any opportunity. No matter how well a job was done they could always find a problem with it.

The ship spent two weeks crossing the Atlantic. Our first port visit was Palma. This was my third visit to the city, and it was becoming as familiar as my hometown. Stress within the division was another reason I used to justify my activities, as I made a direct trip to the red light district.

"Hey Diaz, you want to go alley cattin' with me?" I asked.

We were in the shop watching TV. He laughed and said, "Come on, you know I don't do that kind of stuff. Besides, I got duty today; I'll go out with you tomorrow."

"How about you, Goom?"

AO3 Roland "Goomer" Augustine was a Filipino from Hawaii who hardly spoke more than two sentences a day. From under the ship's ball cap pulled down to his eyes, he muttered, "Okay."

Felicia and I were writing again, but to me that was no guarantee of anything. I knew God could take her away from me at anytime and probably would. It had been a year and a half since my last prostitute, so I felt I had been "good" long enough. A taxi dropped Goomer and me off in the familiar maze of run down bars and brothels behind the cathedral.

Before long, a woman tried to proposition us. Her short bleached hair made her look like the drug addict from two years before. While she was speaking, my eyes locked onto a cute girl with dark hair playing four square with some school children. She looked like a high school student except she was not wearing a uniform. I wasn't sure if she was a street girl, so I approached her cautiously. Not wanting to offend her if I was wrong, the only thing I could think of to say was, "Hi."

She looked up at me and pointed to the fleabag hotel we were next to and asked, "Que usted desea ir arriba con me? ... Upstairs with me?"

"Yes."

"Si?"

"Yeah. Si."

I gave the money to a pimp working behind the front desk. The lobby was decorated with tacky Christmas ornaments and tinsel, and a small tree sat in a corner. The girl led me upstairs and into a room where it was cold enough to see our breath.

She turned on a portable heater, then pointed at me and asked, "Cuales su nombre?"

"I don't understand," I said awkwardly.

"Nombre," she repeated.

It took me a minute to catch on. "My name? Jake. And yours?"

"Juanita." She held up her hands, raised her fingers one at a time then pointed at me again. "Cual es su edad?"

I held up ten fingers twice then five and asked, "And how old are you?"

She raised all her fingers twice.

None of the others had cared enough to ask anything about me. I came out of there feeling guilty and ashamed, but still telling myself there was nothing I could do. Like the others, I felt a strange bonding towards her. By showing a little kindness she really got to me. I tried to think of her as just a worthless prostitute, but couldn't. Goomer waited outside for me. That night I prayed for forgiveness, but the next day I was back in Blood Alley looking for Juanita.

She was locking up her small car at a street curb when I found her. Wil Diaz was with me and acted as my interpreter.

"Ask her if she remembers me," I told Diaz.

"Usted recuerda a este individuo?" he said to her.

"Seguro, lo recuerdo."

"She does."

"Ask her if she's working," I said.

"Usted esta trabajando?"

"Si."

Juanita took my hand and led me back to the brothel. My theory that an artificial relationship was better than none proved false long ago, but saying good-bye was absolutely gut wrenching. What really made things painful was knowing I meant nothing to her; I was just one of a score of men passing through.

When we were through, we stood at the front steps of the hotel looking at each other.

"My ship leaves tomorrow and I'll probably never see you again. I wish you could come with me," I said.

She shrugged her shoulders and slowly shook her head with a smile. I was too embarrassed to have Diaz translate, so we just waved good-bye.

The next morning I had duty. When I awoke, my crotch felt like it was packed in fiberglass insulation. I ran into the head to investigate. The infected area looked as if it were covered with dozens of mosquito bites.

Oh no, I thought, *it's finally caught up with me.* Again, I asked God for forgiveness and promised Him I would never go into another brothel. I had no idea how I'd be able to keep such an unrealistic vow. That afternoon the bumps were gone and the itching stopped. I thought whatever it had been was now gone and there was nothing to worry about. But it would come back later to haunt me.

• • •

When the ship left Spain, McKay became the first of the veterans to kiss up to the Dastardly Duo. One of his airmen saw me in the gym during work hours and told him about it. In order to get in good with the new chiefs he'd rat on anyone, including me. McKay had gone to the gym with me several times during the war cruise when he was the night check supervisor.

The Duo made me work days so I could be watched.

I began reading my Bible regularly. Everyone had been issued one during the war, and it came with a desert camouflage cover. The ship was scheduled to visit Israel in March, and I wanted to study the country's history. Several of us lounged around the shop while the ship maneuvered into Naples. Diaz and I were the petty officers in charge. AN Ted Cook was thumbing through his own Desert Storm Bible and threw a question out to no one in particular, "I wonder what the Bible says about swearing."

The AOs sitting around in their ragged flight deck uniforms paid no attention to him. My memory went back to my years in Christian schools. I remembered being taught about the power of the tongue. I opened my Bible and read aloud James 3:6-9:

> And the tongue is like a fire. It is a world of wrong, occupying its place in our bodies and spreading evil through our whole being. It sets on fire the entire course of our existence with the fire that comes to it from hell itself.

Man is able to tame and has tamed all other creatures,
wild animals and birds, reptiles and fish. But no one
has ever been able to tame the tongue. It is evil and
uncontrollable, full of deadly poison. We use it to give
thanks to our Lord and Father and also to curse our fellow
man, who is created in the likeness of God.

My shipmates looked at me in a silent state of shock. Cook
laughed and said, "Wow! Where did that come from? I just
asked a simple question, and you bowl me over with that."

"It's from the book of James," I said. "It means you can't
pray to God one minute then turn around and cuss somebody
out the next. Because we're all made in God's image."

Everyone pondered my words, everyone except Diaz. He
took his reclining feet down from the forklift desk, pointed a
finger at me and said, "You know, everyday I see you up here
reading that Bible, and now you're preaching to these guys. But
I know what you do in port."

His words knocked the wind out of me. He was still a
friend, but he was showing me for what I was—a hypocrite.
I didn't even try to defend myself. Everyone continued with
what they were doing.

The ship spent the holidays in Naples, where the Navy's
sixth fleet headquarters was located. To the south, Mount
Vesuvius appeared to rise out of the sea and pierce the clouds
with its narrow snow-capped peak. It was terribly cold the
whole time, and the city was filthy. According to the lifers,
the place had been cleaned up. All the buildings were old and
covered with years of dirt and black residue. A medieval castle
sitting on a hill overlooked the waterfront.

Naples had a bad reputation throughout the fleet. It
sounded similar to Palma's Blood Alley, but on a grander scale.
Several lifers talked about a fat old prostitute who was called
"Humpty Dumpty" because she sat on a brick wall across from

the main gate of the American air station. It was rumored she had been there since the end of World War II. All the brothels were located within the off-limits area. The shore patrol, wearing white caps and peacoats and twirling their billy clubs, routinely walked by the area. On Christmas Day I had duty, but since everything ashore was closed, nobody went on liberty anyway, and I had to wait two hours in line for dinner. Two days later, Diaz and I went on a whirlwind tour of Rome. My friend was almost detained by the Swiss Guards for pretending to be intoxicated at the Vatican.

• • •

The ship's next stop was at Suda Bay on the island of Crete. The village was not capable of taking in the entire crew of an American aircraft carrier, so only a third of the ship was allowed to go ashore each day. All my buddies had duty on my liberty day, so I was stuck with a young recruit named Sal Alonso, who had just graduated from a high school in New York City the previous summer. He had the addiction bad.

As we walked off the ferryboat, Alonso said to me, "Porter, take me to a whorehouse."

"What did you call me?" I snapped.

"I mean, Petty Officer Porter. Could you take me to a whorehouse?" he repeated meekly.

"I'm only kidding," I smiled. "Call me Jake. What makes you think I can find one for you?"

"Well, you know? I hear you and the other guys talking about them. I thought maybe you could show me where to go," said Alonso, looking up at me.

"How? I've never been here before."

He kept looking at me with wide brown eyes. I turned to watch the fishing boats in the small harbor and thought, *What would I do if I found one?* I turned back to him and said, "Okay, I'll help you find one, but I'm not going in."

"All right."

The town had a large red-light district, but all the establishments were closed. The white stucco houses literally had red lights by the entrances. Sailors promenading down the narrow streets became more upset each time a brothel turned them away. It was particularly frustrating for them to see the girls watching them from the upper windows. Sitting at the corner of one brothel was a large tomcat with dirty orange fur. He was filthy, but content with his environment while calmly licking a forepaw.

How appropriate, I thought. *Here I am training a new alley cat who wants to learn from the master. Well I don't want to be the master. I wish I could get my virginity back and be totally naïve about these matters.*

A week later, we were in Athens. It was the largest city the America would visit and it swallowed the crew like New York had. My supervisor, Bob Schofield, took me on a tour of most of the ruins. From atop the steep hill where the Acropolis sat, Bob took samples.

"Make sure no one's watching," he said while trying to decide which piece of ancient stone he wanted to pocket. "After sixteen years in the Navy, I bet I've got half the Roman Empire scattered across my backyard in Cape May."

"These aren't Roman, they're Greek," I reminded him.

"What's the difference?"

Growing tired of sightseeing, we entered a tavern and ordered a couple of beers. Before my first sip, a woman wearing an expensive black dress rubbed against me and put an arm around my shoulders. Another one did the same to Bob.

"Would you care to buy something for the ladies?" asked the barkeep. He had short greasy hair parted in the middle, a handlebar mustache, and a gap in his front teeth. While wiping a glass with a dishtowel, he smiled and waited for us to order more drinks.

The ladies weren't prostitutes, they were champagne girls; their job was to get a customer to spend his last dime, then dump him when he did. My lust was controllable when faced with a scam. I gave the barkeep a hard look so he could see I wasn't amused, and said, "No way. Now get them away from me!"

The smile drained from the barkeep's face, and he put the glass back on a shelf.

"You just screwed yourself, buddy," Bob told him.

We finished the beers and walked out of there without leaving a tip. Not even looking at the ladies was a big accomplishment for me.

The next day was different. Wil Diaz, Kevin Kelleher and I wandered through the city's side streets. We didn't have a set agenda, so we walked block after block, peering into the large plate glass windows to see what was on display. I was bored until I looked into one window and saw that the items displayed were women. As we continued our walk, we passed several hotel lobbies that were set up the same way. My friends weren't interested, but once I discovered those brothels I could think of nothing else. I remembered promising God after the episode in Palma that I would never enter one again, but the old temptation was back. I reasoned I had broken other promises to God, so what was one more?

At the next one, I said to my friends, "Hey guys, I'm going inside."

"You're going in one of those places?" asked Kevin.

"Man, he goes in those places all the time," laughed Wil.

"All right, we'll wait for you," said Kevin.

Inside the lobby there were three girls dressed like they were going to a job interview, and reading magazines. I walked up to the front desk where the hotel's procurer greeted me.

"May I help you?"

"Yeah."

"Would you like a room?"

I nodded.

The man quoted me a price, and I gave him a handful of multi-colored paper drachmas.

"Adonia," he said to one of the girls.

The girl was wearing a white blouse and gray skirt with matching jacket. She got up from her chair and led me up stairs. Inside the room, she began to undress. She was a beauty with straight black hair, and normally I would've given into my lust at that point, but something stopped me. I kept thinking of Felicia and Sophia, and a voice of clarity spoke within my head. *How low can you go? What about the promise you made to the Lord? Remember the promise?*

"I can't," I blurted out.

The girl didn't understand me and kept undressing.

"I'm sorry, I can't do this."

She still didn't understand.

Finally, I put my jacket back on and walked out of the room. This time she understood and became offended. Loud Greek profanities echoed through the hall and down the stairway.

"It's not you. I want to, but can't," I told her, but it made no difference. Her pretty face turned red with an ugly scowl, and she held up painted fingernails like claws.

I ran down the stairs before she could get dressed, and the pimp came out from behind his desk and asked, "What's the matter?"

"I just changed my mind, that's all."

"Would you prefer another girl?"

"No, there's nothing wrong the girl. I've just changed my mind." I wondered if I'd have to fight this guy to get my money back. The girl was now charging down the stairs, and I readied to fight them both. The pimp didn't want any trouble, though. He told the girl to stay put and he handed me my money.

Praise God! It was the last brothel I ever went into, but I still had a rough road ahead.

My buddies were surprised to see me out of there so soon and kidded me about it. I didn't care about their jesting; I had proven something to myself. Even though righteous living was still a long way off for me, I came out of there feeling good instead of guilty.

In another brothel that day, there was a pimp who didn't believe in refunds. Some crew members smashed a window with his face and hurled his body across the lobby like a sack of laundry. The offenders went to the brig, and the captain declared all brothels off limits. There was no changing my mind; the shore patrol saw to that.

•   •   •

From Athens the ship sailed to Antalya, Turkey and then to Haifa, Israel. I could hardly believe I was going to visit the Holy Land. At fleet landing, there was a large banner that read, "Welcome to Israel." Shore patrol and Israeli soldiers mingled together as uninterested Jewish and Arab civilians passed by. The place was clean and lacked that "third world stench." Kevin, Wil, Adam Sharpe and I walked around together on the first day. We were impressed with the drinks and food.

At the Church of the Holy Sepulchre in Jerusalem a set of steep steps led to the top of Mt. Calvary. On top was a chapel. The chapel was divided in two; a painted line separated the two halves. One half was Roman Catholic and the other was Greek Orthodox. The aroma of sweet burning incense filled my nostrils. Near the dividing line was a rectangular hole lined with brass. This was supposed to mark where the Cross had been erected. I was literally at the foot of the Cross, but I was still burdened with my sins of immorality and rebellion. My own day of crucifixion had not yet arrived.

During a tour of the Lake Galilee area, we were taken to a

large facility, which cut and polished diamonds. I went into the place thinking there was no way I was going to buy one. The plant knocked fifty percent off the merchandise for American servicemen. Even I couldn't pass up a deal like that, so I bought Felicia an engagement ring. I knew it was crazy buying a ring for a woman I hadn't met.

The original itinerary for the cruise had the ship scheduled for port visits at Marseille, Alexandria, and Istanbul. In his daily address to the crew, the captain informed us that that plan had been cancelled. We would be heading south through the Suez Canal, with port visits to be announced at a later time. The crew nearly cried. Nobody wanted to go back to the Red Sea. I wasn't sure how I was going to endure the tense atmosphere of G-1. Thus far, our time spent at sea had been no longer than two weeks at a time. The hard line the CPOs had taken at the start of the cruise had not subsided. We were working in a pressure cooker.

A murderous hatred festered within me. I hated the senior petty officers, I hated the chiefs, and I hated that jellyfish Lieutenant Rivers who refused to take charge. I wasn't sure I could make it to my separation date of September 13. I cried out to God and asked Him to help. Was there anyway I could get out early with an Honorable Discharge? To my surprise, I received an answer.

A few days later, while the ship was slowly sailing south in the Red Sea, Kevin Kelleher approached me in the berthing. "Porter, have you heard they're giving early outs because of the cut backs?"

"What?" I said, surprised. "Where did you hear this?"

"They were talking about it in the shop. They'll let you out up to ninety days early. All you gotta do is put in a request chit and run it through the chain of command."

After reporting to work, I went straight up the ladder leading to the division office. I asked the LPO about the early out rumor, and he confirmed it was real. He handed me a request chit, which I filled out and handed back to him. Two days later I was told to report to the weapons office. There, the department CPO handed the chit back to me and said, "Approved."

I stared at it in disbelief, but it had all the necessary signatures. My new date of release was June 12, 1992, just eight days after we were to arrive in Norfolk. The end was finally in sight.

When the ship entered the Indian Ocean, the temperature rose. In late March, the America returned to the Persian Gulf. The evening before our first visit to the United Arab Emirates capital of Abu Dhabi, Lt. Rivers held a personnel inspection at the bomb farm. The division lined up into two ranks, wearing our best dungarees. The lieutenant put on a tough look for the sake of the Dastardly Duo; they stood by themselves nodding their approval. *Who's working for whom?* I wondered.

Lt. Rivers went over each man with a fine-toothed comb. (It was the first time I'd ever seen the lieutenant in pressed khakis. His uniforms were usually baggy and wrinkled.) He told the sailor of any "hits" he found, and the LPO would write them on the tablet in his clipboard. When it was my turn, his face was about half an inch from mine as he squinted through his wire frame glasses. After nearly a full minute, he said, "I think you should start shaving a little closer, Porter."

How serious could it be if you had to stand that close for that long? I thought. The absurdity of those ridiculous inspections was driving me insane.

After leaving the Persian Gulf, the ship spent the month of May making the long voyage home. While in the Red Sea, tensions within the division mounted. Chief Beavins wrote up Greg Parker for a trivial incident that resulted in his demotion. I was already under a lot of stress for the upcoming annual 3M inspection.

I spent most of the day on the flight deck while the ship passed through the Suez Canal. It was the last time I'd see it. We crossed the Mediterranean without stopping. The ship anchored briefly at Rota, Spain before it started across the Atlantic. Ten days later it anchored off Bermuda while the 3M inspectors were flown aboard by helicopter. The inspectors were no-nonsense chiefs from COMNAVAIRLANT (Commander, Naval Air Force, Atlantic Fleet). They would come aboard every American carrier in the Atlantic Ocean once a year and randomly select a signed-off piece of preventive maintenance from every work center. This meant five inspections for G-1. Since I was the only one in DC who did the maintenance, I was their lucky winner. By the end of the inspection my nerves were shot and I had psoriasis on my elbows.

With the end of the cruise in sight, I was proud of having made only two visits to a brothel. For me that was real progress. I was looking forward to marrying Felicia and moving on to a civilian career.

9
DISCHARGED

He who finds a wife finds what is good and receives favor from the
Lord. Proverbs 18:22

THE LEGAL OFFICE POINTED me in the right direction for
obtaining immigration forms for Felicia. The first INS (Immigration and Naturalization Service) form I received required
a passport-type photograph of me. I found a photographer's
mate at the ship's lab and told him what I was trying to do. He
seemed sympathetic and said he would give it a try.

On June 4 the ship returned to Norfolk. Two days later a
pink sign-out sheet was given to me that required signatures
from various offices on the ship. For three days I wandered
throughout the carrier visiting the legal office, education
office, damage control central, weapons office, library, chaplain's office, personnel office, disbursing office, and others.
Every person I spoke with said it was up to someone else in
the office to sign and they were out for the moment. Chiefs
and officers didn't want to sign until required signatures from
persons of a lower rank were obtained.

The day finally arrived. On June 12 I felt like a child
on Christmas morning. The personnel office gave me my
discharge papers and a pink ID card. I held the DD-214 form
in front of my face and smiled. I was given an honorable
discharge and awarded a Good Conduct Discharge. At G-1, I

made a final check of my personal items and said good-bye to the men with whom I had served.

I carried my solid seabag up to the hangar deck. It was heavy as bricks. At the after brow, I said to the chief of the watch, "Requesting permission to go ashore."

He looked at my new ID card and discharge papers. "What are your plans now?" he asked.

"Well, I'm trying to get into a police academy in California," I answered.

He handed the documents back to me. "Okay, permission granted, and good luck."

I took three steps, did a right face movement toward the flag, and then walked off the USS America for good. Wil Diaz drove me to the Airport. We shook hands and told each other good-bye. As the plane lifted off I looked at the huge shipyards scattered about the Tide Water area, then leaned back for the long trip to Montana.

• • •

The excitement of leaving the Navy was short lived. Once I was back in the house of my parents, I immediately felt out of place. They had not changed, but I had. I flopped on the bed of my old room and looked at the ceiling. Four years earlier I had been in the same spot the night before shipping out to boot camp. "Now what?" I asked out loud.

The future looked grim. I tried to switch back to the frame of mind I had been in while a criminal justice student. While working for the campus police, my fellow students and I had aspired to be cops like Joe Friday or Dirty Harry. After digging out two group photos of the campus police, some worthless certificates I had framed, and old homework assignments, I psyched myself up enough to drive back to Santa Rosa. The academy there didn't accept me.

Just before I made my trip to California, Felicia called me.

It was exciting to hear her voice for the first time, even though it was hard to understand her English. She called again shortly after I returned and did so about every week throughout June and July. The American Embassy in Manila would not grant her a tourist visa. I decided to go over there and marry her. When she called again I told her of my plans. She was thrilled, but speechless.

The cost of the plane ticket and my passport just about cleaned up all of my severance pay. I drove to Seattle and put my car into long-term parking. In the morning, I boarded a 747 for the ten-hour flight to Seoul; from there it was another three hours to the Philippines. My heart rate increased as the plane descended on its final approach to Manila. I was finally going to meet Felicia, but I was plagued with doubts. *What if she changes her mind when she sees me?* I asked myself. The fear of rejection was stronger than ever. I was afraid this would be another dead end like all the others. Except this time I had gambled everything. All of my money had gone into the fees for various INS forms, the ring, and my airfare. All that remained of my severance pay was in my wallet.

The inside of the Ninoy Aquino Airport was different than those in the states. There were no throngs of excited relatives or cultural exhibits decorating the walls. The long corridor leading to customs was void of any decor, and grim faced soldiers, with submachine guns watched the passengers. I was the only white person there and everyone stared at me.

My seabag was inspected by a friendly woman who wanted to make small talk, but I just wanted to get out of there and find Felicia. Even in the main terminal there were no people except airline employees milling around the ticket counters. Just in front of the doors leading outside, was a middle-aged man who approached me.

"Are you Jake Porter?" he asked.

"Yes."

"Follow me, please."

Outside it was dark, but the heat and humidity was the worse I had felt since crossing the Equator. Streaks of perspiration ran down the sides of my face. Along the street in front of the terminal, taxis picked up and dropped off passengers. Just beyond the street, was a low metal barricade that separated the terminal complex from a large crowd of waiting friends and relatives. The man led me to a group who were watching me anxiously.

"Here they are," he said.

They? I was expecting to meet one person. Lights from the airport were shining in my eyes and making it impossible for me to tell which one was Felicia. Eventually, someone pushed her to the front. Felicia was even more nervous than I. She was thin and petite with wavy black hair hanging just above her shoulders.

"Hello," she said shyly.

One of her relatives owned a jeepny that everyone piled into. Two benches were mounted inside the jeepny's bed where all of us took a seat. Felicia introduced me to the large group, which included some of her brothers, nieces, cousins, and friends. As the jeepny made its way through the bustling streets of Manila, the group spoke to one another in Tagalog.

The house was located on an old army base called Fort Bonifacio in Makati, the business district of Metro Manila. It was a simple structure with plywood walls and concrete floor. Inside there were even more people. Felicia introduced me to her parents and younger sister. Her mother brought Sophia out to meet me. She was only eight months old and did not have a clue as to what was happening.

A long table was laid with more food than a church potluck. Felicia served me a plate of spaghetti with buttered bread. While I ate, the men questioned me about my plans.

Felicia had reserved a suite for us on the seventh floor of

a hotel in Makati. The place had a kitchen, a living room, a bathroom, and a bedroom with twin beds. I climbed into one of the beds and laid there most of the night listening to the air conditioner. I had been awake for over twenty-four hours, but couldn't sleep. Felicia had not shown much enthusiasm, and I started to believe I had struck out again.

My doubts about her feelings disappeared that afternoon when I gave her the diamond ring. She gave me a big kiss, then excitedly put the ring on her finger. It was a loose fit for her, but that didn't stop her from showing it to her family members back at the house. When she kissed me I saw fireworks. It was my first genuine kiss from a woman and it meant more to me than all the others.

The next day, August 7, 1992 we were married in our hotel suite by a justice of the peace. A few of Felicia's relatives acted as witnesses. The ceremony was brief and to the point and when it was over the hotel's room service brought up platters of the local cuisine. When lunch was finished, we started the long bureaucratic nightmare that was to haunt us for the next year.

Two nights later, Felicia and I were lying in bed listening to the tropical downpour. She asked me, "Have you ever been with any other women before?"

The question took me by surprise, and I tried to form a truthful answer that didn't reveal any details. I was overcome with shame and began sobbing.

"What's the matter?" she asked. "Are you okay?"

"Yes, I have," I whispered.

"It's okay, we don't have to talk about it."

I cried and couldn't stop for several minutes. I'd never ever done that before.

When the time came to fly home, Felicia went with me to the airport, but she was not allowed inside the terminal. It was the most difficult good-bye I'd ever gone through. She returned to the hotel and tearfully packed her suitcase. At the North-West ticket counter I checked in and started walking to the gate. Just before the security checkpoint, I had to pay a forty-dollar "terminal fee." Then I was flat broke and making an international flight. I didn't even know how I was going to get my car out of long-term parking.

When I arrived in Seattle, I found the cool air refreshing. My parents' credit card number was enough to secure the release of my car, and I began the long drive to Polson. While driving north on Highway 93 in Montana I became overwhelmed with anxiety in regards to getting a job and when I would actually get to see Felicia again. Already I missed her terribly and I had not even made it home yet.

•   •   •

When I walked into the house that night I was relieved to find an unemployment check from the state. This provided a little breathing room while I tested for various law enforcement agencies. I phoned and wrote to agencies all over the country and I tested in four states. In each case, I either totally bombed the test or missed it by a hair. Over the next year I became increasingly discouraged, and with each failure my self confidence plummeted. Besides filling out numerous employment packets, I was also handling immigration forms that required a fee of a hundred dollars or more.

The frustration of fighting the government and trying to get a job was taking its toll on me. Every night I was drinking heavily, either at a local bar or from a bottle I kept hidden in my closet. When driving on one of my many trips I would listen to hard rock tapes with depressing or angry lyrics, because they expressed exactly how I felt. As time went on, I became aware that I was imposing on my parents. On Thanksgiving I did not want to come out of my room because I felt like an unwanted guest whom my parents were obligated to invite. A couple of weeks later my dad came into the den where I was watching a movie, and he told me I needed to get a job, any job.

My car spun out of control while driving to a test in Colorado. It was the middle of December, and most of the highway was covered with ice. I was calm while the car spun like a top on the icy interstate. Since I had passed several tractor-trailers I was hoping one would crash into the car and kill me. The car came to a sudden stop on the median, which was covered with about two feet of snow. I was still alive, but disappointed. "Oh God, please let me die and end this agony," I pleaded.

In May there was a job vacancy at the Lake County Jail in Polson. Being a corrections officer never interested me, but I thought it could lead to a deputy's position. My interview was with the under-sheriff and the jail supervisor. The supervisor wanted me for the job, but the under-sheriff gave it to somebody else.

On June 12, 1993, one year since I had left the Navy, I was still living at home without a job; I could hardly stand to look at myself in the mirror. On Father's Day I received a phone call from the jail supervisor who said if I wanted the job on a part time basis to get down there right away. Excitedly I hung up the phone and drove to the courthouse.

It became the worst job of my life. The reality of the setting did not coincide with my expectations of a small town jail. I thought being part of a three or four man staff watching over a few prisoners who were there to sober up would be a stress-free job. I was surprised to find five cell blocks crammed with inmates dressed in orange uniforms. Public intoxication was the least of their crimes. The jail population represented every felony and misdemeanor in the law books. What really unsettled me was that only one jailer worked per shift, and the shifts were twelve hours long. Friday and Saturday nights were different, when the part timer would come in and help from 8:00 P.M. to 4:00 A.M. The part time jailer usually got the same or more hours than the full time people, because he had to take over for those who called in sick.

The American Embassy in Manila continued to play its games. I prayed for answers, but received nothing. Out of desperation I scraped together money left over from my unemployment checks and what little I had made at the jail and bought another ticket to the Philippines.

10
THE CURSE

But if you fail to do this, you will be sinning against the Lord; and you may be sure that your sin will find you out. Numbers 32:23

THE FLIGHT WAS a little different than the previous one. From Spokane I flew to Denver, where I caught a seven-hour flight to Honolulu. It was my first time in Hawaii, but I could not see anything, because it was the middle of the night. After the short layover, I boarded another 747 for an eight-hour flight to Guam. At the airport in Guam, I learned my flight to Manila had been cancelled and it would be three hours until the next one. The delay was especially frustrating because I had no way of calling Felicia who was supposed to meet me at 11:00 A.M.

After the long layover, I boarded a plane for the final leg of the journey. I arrived in Manila around 1:00 P.M. local time. Felicia and one of her brothers had waited for me. I hardly recognized Felicia and it was like meeting her all over again. Sophia was also there; she was walking, but would not let me hold her. The giant tropical sun directly overhead hit me like a sledgehammer. My new shirt was wet within minutes. We made two trips to the embassy that first week, and they finally granted the visa.

By the first week of September, Felicia and I were together in Polson, and my parents warmly welcomed her into the family. My mom put together a large reception for us with old friends and most of the church attending. It was a pleasant month, but things suddenly came crashing down.

Working as a part-time jailer was not going to cover the expenses we were incurring. I swallowed my pride and applied for food stamps and Medicare. We had to move into an apartment for section eight housing, where the rent was based on our incomes and the government paid the rest. During the holiday season, we didn't even have enough money to buy a Christmas tree. When my dad purchased a tree and brought it over, I stayed in the bedroom, too embarrassed to face him. Our dealings with the embassy were not over, either, since we were now trying to get Sophia a visa.

The Navy's financial center sent me a letter saying I owed them four hundred dollars for a check they mistakenly gave me and the account was turned over to a collection agency. Some mistake made by a personnelman on the America ruined my credit for the next seven years and cost all our savings. I wondered where God was and why He was allowing this to happen to me.

At the end of September we learned Felicia was pregnant. My parents were elated, but I was depressed. The last thing I needed was another mouth to feed.

I was in for another shock.

At the medical clinic, I sat in the lobby reading a magazine while Felicia had some tests done. She came out of the office with a confused look on her face.

"The nurse wants to talk with us both," she said. "But I'm not sure why."

Felicia led me into a small room where a lab technician wearing a white jacket was sitting on a black cushioned stool. She introduced herself as Lori and explained to us, in medical terms, about a virus discovered in Felicia's blood. Neither of us quite understood what she was saying.

Lori took off her glasses and said, "Felicia, you have a strain of the herpes virus."

A surge of adrenaline doubled my heart rate because I suddenly knew where this was going. My dark hidden secrets were starting to surface right there in the doctor's office. Felicia still looked confused.

Lori explained further. "Felicia, you have a sexually trans-mitted disease. It is something you contract from sexual inter-course with a man who already has it. Have you been with another man?"

When Felicia finally understood, a look of pain and betrayal spread across her face. "No, I never did anything like that," she said then looked at me for an explanation.

I told the lab tech about Felicia having been raped and hoped the cause could be linked to that incident. However, I knew I was the one. I remembered my last visit to that brothel in Spain, and the mysterious rash I had the following morning.

Things became worse when Dr. Gloria Johnson came in. "Right now the herpes is very active in your uterus, and the baby has only a fifty-fifty chance of living."

I could not get out of there fast enough.

In the car, Felicia wanted answers. "I don't understand. How did I get this?"

"Maybe you got it the first time you became pregnant," I offered.

"No! I didn't have this virus when I gave birth to Sophia. How many other women were there?" she insisted.

I wasn't offering any other explanations and remained silent for the rest of the drive. Back at the apartment, I secluded myself in the bedroom and cried out to God, "Why are You allowing this to happen? Didn't I tell You I was sorry about all of those sins, and now You're letting it all out in the open?"

I collapsed to the floor and wept. "Why, God, must my wife suffer and my child's life be in danger for my sin? I don't know what else I can do. How many times can I say I'm sorry? Oh please, just let me die."

· · ·

In February 1994, I was given a full-time spot at the jail. On March 22, I was hired as a part-time police officer for the town of Hot Springs, fifty miles to the west in Sanders County. Felicia and I were working a lot of hours, but there was little money coming in. We were still buying groceries with food stamps and the rent had to be adjusted for every extra dollar we made.

On Easter Sunday Felicia was so sick from the herpes she was not able to have dinner with the family. Dr. Johnson admitted her into the local hospital the following day. My parents were concerned, but I could not bring myself to tell them the true cause of her illness. For those who asked, I said she had a bladder infection. The baby's due date was only a week away, and the herpes was dangerously active. It was essential the virus returned to its dormant condition, and within two days it had.

Felicia was released from the hospital, but returned a week later. On April 19 the doctor induced labor, and Felicia gave birth to Jeffery. A nurse wrapped him in a blue blanket and let me hold him. I gave a silent prayer of thanks. He was a strong, healthy bundle of energy. In November Felicia went back to the Philippines and returned with Sophia who was about to turn three.

As the year wore on, the two jobs started to burn me out. Days off were rare and the hours were long. Felicia had several babysitting and house cleaning jobs, but financially we barely kept our heads above water. I decided to test for some large out-of-state agencies.

When that idea didn't work, I took a hard look at my options, but nothing seemed promising. Then one evening I received a call from Scott Straub in Ohio. It was great to hear from him, and we reminisced about our adventures overseas. I'd forgotten the things I hated about the Navy and found myself thinking of the friends I'd made and the places we'd seen.

That summer I decided I would return to the Navy by going back to college and getting my bachelor's degree. Combined with the college credits I already had, I figured this could be completed in about eighteen months. With a BA degree I'd meet the educational requirements for officer training. Instead of returning as an enlisted man, I'd come back as an ensign so those chiefs would have to call me Sir.

When I received an acceptance letter from the University of Montana, I was excited; my new journey to success was underway. In August 1995 I resigned from the jail. But when the semester started in September, I could tell things were going to get rough. Since I was driving to Missoula five times a week, I would not be able to work the weekends in Hot Springs, so I took a leave of absence. The only money I would be bringing in was four-hundred dollars a month from the G.I. Bill, and that was only good for ten-thousand dollars. When I saw the list of required classes, my spirits sank. It was going to take more than two or three years to complete everything.

The four-hundred dollars a month I was getting paid the rent, and the money Felicia earned covered everything else. Student loans paid the actual cost of school. When my mom asked if we were going to the church family camp, I said we couldn't afford it. However, she persisted and I came up with the money.

• • •

The church families met at a large lodge with surrounding cabins, set in the forest east of Flathead Lake. We were fed three square meals a day and listened to some superb teaching. I even enjoyed the simple things, like sitting at the campfire and drinking hot chocolate while the others sang hymns. Then came the morning Jerry Praetzel taught in the lodge's dining room.

Jerry and Linda had been on staff at the YWAM base in Salem, Oregon and had been the directors at the base in Riggins, Idaho. Then, for the past two and half years they had been living in Polson, while Jerry taught in churches across the USA and Canada.

Jerry's lecture was about God's blessings and curses. As I listened, I became aware of the satanic powers that constantly work against us. Obedience to God brings blessings, but sin brings curses to the third and fourth generations. Deuteronomy 28 lists the signs of a curse: humiliation, barrenness or unfruitfulness, mental and physical sickness, family breakdown, poverty, defeat, oppression, failure, and suicide or untimely death. Poverty, failure, and suicide stood out like neon signs!

There was something there for everyone. Many recalled going to fortunetellers, playing with Ouija boards, or having a relative in the freemasons where blood oaths are sworn. When we engage in sin, it's like making a deal with the devil, and he isn't going to just walk away when we change our minds. The curses not only come from sins of immorality, but also ethical sin, anti-Semitism, legalism, carnality, apostasy, theft, perjury, gossiping, withholding tithes, selfish prayers, and more.

In my own family, there were past incidents of suicide and early death. This spirit of suicide, which followed me like a shadow, had been lingering in my family for generations. At the end of his talk, Jerry invited those who wished for prayer to come forward. Nearly everyone did, including me. As Jerry and other church leaders laid hands on me I openly cried in front of my parents and everyone else. My mom and dad knew things were tough on me. I could see every dream and ambition slip through my fingers like sand as Jerry commanded the demonic forces to flee from me. For the first time in many years, my spirit ached to be reunited with Christ.

When it was over, I felt rejuvenated and there was an excitement about reading the Bible. After we returned to our apartment, I read the Word every day. Even though the scriptures gave me temporary comfort, though, I did not understand what I was reading. I had been correct in recognizing my failures as being attacks from satanic forces, but I was wrong in assuming it was because of sins committed by my ancestors. It was my sins that made me a slave to the devil, and he was not going to let me go so easily.

•   •   •

Now that I had rededicated my life to Jesus, I saw an open road to success. I figured the family curse of failure and suicide would no longer have an effect on me. For the next month, I read the Bible and prayed daily, but spiritually I felt dry as a desert. Without any kind of warning, I was hit with an inner turmoil that would not abate. The dark suicidal depression within me was not just another bout; it would not go away. My sleep was restless, and in the morning I was angered for having lived to see another day. It took every ounce of energy to get out of the door and drive the seventy miles to school.

Even more terrifying, I became possessed with a spirit of concupiscence. It went far beyond normal sexual lust. I had one porn video I watched once or twice a week after the kids had gone to bed. Inside my seabag was a short stack of magazines I had collected from the ship, and I looked through them several times a week. However, they were all of the "soft-core" type, and they didn't do anything for me.

In my mind, I constantly recalled every sexual incident, no matter how slight, with every woman I'd been with. While walking across the university campus it was impossible not to look and fantasize. Physically, I never cheated on my wife, but mentally I did a thousand times. I still loved her, but what I was dealing with had nothing to do with love. Despite my hunger for sexual stimulation, I became frigid with Felicia. I would become detached, like I was watching myself on television, and felt nothing when she became hurt by my rejection.

Added to that, I was becoming increasingly paranoid. I wasn't sure what I was afraid of, but I felt my family and fellow church members were somehow conspiring against me. One day I was driving with the family through town and I noticed another car behind us. I was sure it was trying to follow me. Rather than drive directly to our apartment, I sped up, turned into the church parking lot, and stopped behind the tool shed. After a few minutes, when I thought it was safe, I drove back home. My dad had been parked at the apartment and saw us speed by.

Felicia was becoming concerned about me and was seriously considering going back to the Philippines with the kids. In January she told my parents about my peculiar behavior and asked my dad to speak with me. He came over one evening and sat with me in the living room. He just flat out asked, "Jake, what's wrong?"

I didn't have an answer, so I said, "It's school. No matter how hard I try I'm still failing my tests and I keep getting poor grades. There's no money in the bank. . . . You know, stuff like that."

A week later, I received a phone call from Jerry Praetzel who wanted to meet with me. He came over and asked how things were going. I told him not good and mentioned the bad grades and lack of money.

"How's your Christian life?" Jerry asked.

"I've tried so hard to do what I'm suppose to, but things just keep getting worse."

Jerry sat on our old yellow couch and thought for a minute.

"You know Jake, sometimes we have unresolved sin in our lives, which will hamper our relationship with God. He wants to bless us, but can't until those sins are dealt with. You follow me?"

"Yeah, I think so." I didn't have a clue as to what he meant.

He told me that the teaching seminars he gives at churches across the country deal with rooting out those hidden sins. The teachings were called Plumb Line. A plumb line, or plumb bob, is a rope with a lead weight attached to one end. It's used to determine if a wall is vertical. I saw the analogy and realized my spiritual life was not vertical.

"I'm working on a Plumb Line for our church," he continued. "I would like you to consider attending it."

"Okay."

My grades for that first semester were three Ds and an F. The university sent me a letter saying I was on academic probation and if my GPA did not improve after the second semester I would be suspended. As a child I had always gotten poor grades, but I associated that with being lazy and a lack of effort. That was certainly not the case now. Then one afternoon, while driving home in the Ford Bronco I had bought the previous spring, the engine threw a rod.

What else can go wrong? I tried to keep my composure. The poverty, the failure, the temptations, and now this; I knew it was all related, and that I was under an intense demonic attack. "Why are You allowing this to happen, God? What else must I do to gain Your favor?"

The following Sunday, Jerry announced in church he would be holding a Plumb Line next weekend for those who were interested. "Do you want to go?" Felicia whispered to me.

I was afraid of going, but knew I had to. "Yeah, I guess we should."

After the service, Jerry came over to us.

"We'll be there," I said.

Jerry smiled. "Good, I was hoping you would."

11
THE CONFESSION

Therefore confess your sins to each other and pray for each other so that you may be healed. The prayer of a righteous man is powerful and effective. James 5:16

ON FRIDAY NIGHT Felicia and I had dinner at a restaurant before going to the church, but I could hardly eat. I was overcome with nausea. Going to the church and throwing up in front of everyone did not appeal to me, so I considered going home. A calming voice within me said it was not a physical ailment and I should proceed to the Plumb Line.

Since my Bronco was still in the shop, I drove to the church in my dad's green '72 Chevy pickup. As soon as I entered the doorway the feeling of sickness left me. The small group of four couples and two women met in the conference room. Jerry had set up a lightweight aluminum easel that held a white marking board. With green and red pens he drew a diagram of where God wanted us to be spiritually and where most of us probably were. The plumb line was either too far to the left or the right, but it needed to be perfectly vertical. One side of the line represented addictions, such as drug use, alcohol abuse, compulsive sex, pornography, gambling, or overeating; these ultimately replace God in our lives. The other side was rebellion, which is sin we intentionally commit knowing it is in violation of God's law.

That first session lasted about an hour and it was basically a summary of what we were to learn over the next two days. As Jerry briefly explained the material, everyone seemed to understand what we were in for, except me. I was not sure where I fit in. Even though I had committed some of those sins, they were in the past and I had prayed for forgiveness.

Late that night Felicia suddenly awoke from a troubling nightmare. She had dreamed of a voodoo witch doctor cutting the head off a chicken and sprinkling its blood on her.

The next morning everyone met at the Praetzel's house on King's Point, which juts out from the west shore of Flathead Lake. Jerry spent the entire day elaborating on what he had outlined the previous evening, and Linda prepared lunch for a dozen people. It was a lot of information for me to take in, and I tried earnestly to sort out what was applicable for my life. One thing sinking in quickly was that God hates sin. Whether we are in denial that it exists, or involved in open rebellion, He cannot dwell where sin is present.

For most men, deep-rooted sin has a sexual nature. It usually starts when we are young boys through some voyeuristic form such as pornography or secretly watching a woman undress. I recalled doing both at a very young age. It was frightening how I could recall those images so vividly from a time in my life when everything else was difficult to remember. Like drugs, pornography leaves its user craving for more. The user will struggle with lust even after he is married. Many of those men will act upon that lust during their adolescent years. Getting married is no guarantee they will not act out in some kind of deviant behavior as adults.

On the other side are the women who are often the victims of lust. They are the targets for rapists, molesters, and voyeurs. The victims are not responsible for the actions of their attackers, but they are often in sin for unforgiveness. Hatred is understandable, but the transgressions made against us by our fellow human beings pale in comparison to the sins we have committed against the Lord. We deserve hell and eternal separation from God, but He loves us enough to forgive our sins. However, He cannot forgive us if we will not forgive others. If someone forgave me a billion dollar debt, shouldn't I be willing to waive a hundred dollars owed to me?

I still was not sure why so many problems plagued my life. Jerry seemed to be saying I should ask God to forgive my sins and forgive those who have wronged me. *But I've done that,* I thought to myself. After realizing I had sinned, I prayed for forgiveness every time. Surely He wouldn't hold forgotten sins against me.

There was still more. God does not just listen to our words, He also examines our hearts. Pride interferes with genuine humility. God not only wants us to confess our sins, but to do it with a humble heart and broken spirit (Ps. 51:17 & I Pet. 5:6). *So how do I humble myself enough so that my prayers are effective?* I wondered.

Jerry explained why Catholics go to confession. Revealing our dirty secrets to other Christians is a very humbling experience, but it will also hold us accountable. The agenda for the next day was for each of us to confess our sins to the group as mentioned in James 5:16, and the others would pray for our spiritual healing.

In conclusion, Jerry said, "Go home, have a quiet time of prayer, and ask the Lord to reveal any sins He wants you to confess. You may already know what you need to deal with, but He may also remind you of things you've forgotten about. When something comes to mind, get with your spouse and confess to him or her first. That way there'll be no unpleasant surprises tomorrow."

As I drove home I considered what "bad things" I'd done that would be okay to discuss. I'd known Jerry and Linda for twenty years and they were like family to me. Silently I prayed,

Come on God, you know I'm really, really sorry for those dirty sins in my past. So we're all squared away, right?

When we got home I grabbed my Bible, locked myself in the bedroom, and calmly sat at the foot of our bed. I opened the Bible and silently read a few scriptures. After closing it, I took a deep breath and bowed my head. "Okay God, what is it I'm to share with the group tomorrow?" Never had the Holy Spirit jolted me like He did at that moment. I felt as if I were being gripped by a powerful and angry, yet loving force. In my mind's eye—as clear as photographs—were the faces of every prostitute I had been with, and the word "VICTIMS" in bold letters.

I fell to the floor and sobbed for all of them. They were human beings created and loved by the Heavenly Father, and I had used them for my own selfish gratification. "I'm sorry, I'm so sorry," I cried. My spirit was broken, but there was more.

The pictures in my head changed. There were memories going back to my childhood involving the use of pornography, and deviant behavior. "Oh God, I can't talk about all that. Please, not that," I begged.

No audible words were spoken, but the stern presence of the Holy Spirit remained adamant. When I had composed myself, I asked Felicia to come into the room.

"So, is there anything you're supposed to tell me?" she asked.

"Yes. Come on in." I lay on the bed and covered my eyes with a pillow. "Do you remember shortly after we were married, you asked me if I had been with any other women?"

"Yes."

"I told you I had."

"I remember."

The tears started flowing from my eyes and into my ears like they had the first time this subject came up. My throat tightened, but I forced myself to speak.

"They weren't just 'other women.' They were . . . prostitutes."

Somehow, I had managed to say it, but I wasn't sure how
she would react. To my relief, she hugged me and said, "It's all
right. Nothing is going to change between us."

I realized I had not just a wife, but one who was truly a
gift from God. She was a woman I didn't deserve. Even though
I had been with so many other women and had given her
herpes, she still loved me.

•   •   •

The next morning my stomach was tied in knots. We left the
kids with my parents and drove out to King's Point. When we
came to within a mile of the Praetzel's house, Felicia became ill
and had trouble breathing. I knew she'd be all right once we got
there, so I kept driving. As the truck started up an incline, it
lost traction. The wheels spun on a patch of ice and we weren't
going anywhere. I backed the truck down the incline and tried
again. The truck couldn't make it, so we headed back into town
knowing everyone was at the house waiting for us. When we
reversed directions, Felicia immediately felt better.

We returned to my parents' house and took their Oldsmo-
bile, which had front wheel drive. When we turned onto King's
Point, Felicia became ill again and the car would not make it
up the incline.

"Something is trying to keep us from going there," Felicia
said nervously.

Up to that point I hadn't said anything about my suspi-
cions, because I didn't want to sound paranoid. I'd always been
skeptical of people who claimed to have interacted with the
supernatural. However, this on-again, off-again sickness we
had been going through since Friday convinced me that what
was happening to us was real. Demonic forces didn't want us to
attend that final meeting. This bolstered my determination.

"I know. That's why we have to get there," I said.

By moving the right wheels onto the shoulder, where there was some snow and loose gravel, I found the necessary traction to make it over the hill. As we pulled into the Praetzel's driveway, Felicia's mysterious illness went away.

Everyone was sitting in the living room.

"Sorry we're late," I said, "But it's been a crazy morning." We took our seats and Jerry got started.

Between Jerry and Linda was the "hot seat." Whoever was ready to go would sit in the chair and make his or her confession. Afterwards Jerry and Linda would lay hands on the person and pray. "By the way, what's said in this room stays in this room," said Jerry.

I wanted to go first so I could get it over with, but others had the same thing in mind. My anxiety was alleviated a little when the other men confessed sexual sins similar to or worse than mine. It was comforting to know I was not the only one on the planet with this problem. Once they had exposed their secrets and cried a gallon of tears while asking God for forgiveness, they became new men. The change within them was instant, and joy radiated from their faces. They were ready to fulfill the plans God had for them.

Whenever I got my nerve up, somebody else would get to the chair first. Each one looked like a sheep entering the slaughterhouse. At noon we broke for lunch. I was so nervous, I couldn't eat. Instead of having lunch, I went down into the basement bathroom to be alone. I washed my face with cold water and looked into the mirror, trying to reassure myself.

When I returned to the kitchen, Jerry asked, "Has the Lord revealed anything to you?"

Speaking was a major effort, so I just nodded my head.

When the session reconvened in the living room, I stood up and made my way to the chair. All eyes were on me, but there was no turning back.

I sat in the wooden chair and looked at an overhead beam, thus avoiding eye contact with anyone. In a monotone voice, I admitted that even though I had been brought up in a Christian home, where my parents had tried so hard to shield me from negative influences, I still rebelled against God. As early as age eight I was looking at pornographic magazines that a friend of mine had found in his father's closet. Over the next several years the material I dug up was more explicit, which led to inappropriate sexual behavior by my early teens. While in high school, I was turned down by every girl I asked out. I had gone the entire four years without a date. After each rejection I would try to talk myself into committing suicide. In college the rejection continued, and I began searching for brief sexual encounters as a substitute. I explained to the group while in foreign ports with the Navy those encounters became possible with prostitutes. I told them that now I was sure God wanted me to reconcile with Him over those sins of immorality.

Everything was now in the open. When coming to the crux of my admission I had intended to use some euphemism like "bordellos" or "houses of ill repute," but I said "whorehouses." It was an ugly word for an ugly sin, and I could hear the others gasp.

Jerry turned to me and sternly asked, "Jake, about those prostitutes. Do you realize they were probably victims of abuse and were working against their will?"

"I do now." My voice was a whisper.

Jerry continued, "While you were speaking, I suddenly remembered a conversation I had with your grandmother about fifteen years ago. She was telling me about the time your sister died. You said something at that time, didn't you?"

As I answered his question my mind returned to that hot summer morning on June 29, 1970.

"I told my mom I hated Jesus for taking my sister."

"How old were you then?"

"Four."

"Four years old," Jerry said. "You know, I think that's where your rebellion began. Have you ever asked Him to forgive you for saying that?"

"No."

"Why don't you do that now? Ask Christ to forgive you for saying that, and release your sister into His hands."

It took everything within me to keep my voice from choking up. In front of everyone I asked Jesus to forgive me for that hateful statement I had uttered so many years ago. Then I asked forgiveness for my rebellion and acts of immorality.

"I'm getting a word of knowledge," said Jerry as he stood up and grabbed a Bible from a light stand. When he returned, he opened it to Isaiah 54 and read:

> 'For a brief moment I forsook you, but with great compassion I will gather you. In an outburst of anger I hid My face from you for a moment; but with everlasting loving kindness I will have compassion on you,' says the Lord your Redeemer.
>
> 'For this is like the days of Noah to Me; when I swore that the waters of Noah should not flood the earth again, so I have sworn that I will not be angry with you, nor will I rebuke you. For the mountains may be removed and the hills may shake, but My loving kindness will not be removed from you, and My covenant of peace will not be shaken,' says the Lord who has compassion on you.
>
> 'O afflicted one, storm-tossed, and not comforted, behold, I will set your stones in antimony, and your foundations I will lay in sapphires.'

Those words of rebuke, followed by ones of forgiveness and prosperity, caused tears to cascade down my cheeks. Jerry asked the women to act on behalf of those of whom I had taken advantage, and extend their forgiveness to me. Compassionately, all of them gathered around and placed their hands on me, while saying I was forgiven. At that moment I felt myself being released from the bondage of sexual addiction and suicide. The demons finally relinquished their hold on me, and I was filled with inner peace and joy. This was something I had never experienced before. I silently acknowledged that Jesus had saved my life, and I dedicated myself to His service.

One of the ladies was kind enough to say, "If I had known you in high school, I would have gone out with you."

"Thanks," I said, still unable to look anyone in the eye. "But everything's turned out all right. The Lord has blessed me with a wonderful wife."

Everyone agreed.

Before I left the chair, Jerry said, "Okay Jake, you finally got it out of you. Don't worry, you'll never have to tell those things again."

I was extremely relieved to hear that, but neither one of us knew how wrong he was.

In the hymn "O for a Thousand Tongues," Charles Wesley wrote:

> He breaks the power of canceled sin;
> He sets the prisoner free.
> His blood can make the foulest clean;
> His blood availed for me.

I was living proof of that. I felt myself being revived, filled with a new spiritual source. Most of the women waited until the men were finished before taking their turn in the chair. Just as Jerry had taught earlier, most of them, at one time or another, had been victims of sexual abuse and had struggled with forgiveness. The acts they had suffered occurred many years ago in their childhoods, but the wounds were still painful. It was now my turn to intercede for them.

Brothers, cousins, fathers, uncles, and grandfathers had

sexually violated some of the ladies as little girls. One of the women stopped praying and told everyone she had seen an ominous shadow flee the room. I didn't see anything, but I had been feeling this invisible tension all day. There was a sensation of combat in the air.

The whole thing ended about 9:00 P.M. Everyone was physically drained of energy. And I was starving, since I hadn't eaten all day.

• • •

We picked up the kids and returned to our apartment. The atmosphere inside felt like being wrapped in a blanket full of static electricity. After eating some dinner, we got into bed around 10:30. When I turned off the lights, the darkness was blacker than ink. My eyes couldn't adjust to it and the static feeling intensified. Even though we were both exhausted, neither of us could sleep. Two words came to mind, "spiritual warfare." I had heard the term before, but I wasn't sure what it meant. Around midnight, my eyes still hadn't adjusted to the darkness, and Felicia began having problems breathing, again.

Now I was angry. I had intended to "clean house" in the morning, but now I felt there was no time to wait. In the middle of the night I got up, turned the lights on, and began looking for anything that could be connected to demonic activity. I got a box and threw in every pornographic magazine and book. Then I gathered up my entire tape collection of rock music and hauled everything out to the dumpster. I found my only X-rated videotape, stuck it in the VCR, turned on the Disney Channel, and hit the record button. When that was completed, I took my Bible and opened it to Isaiah 54:7-17 and read aloud the promises given to me that day.

In the morning I called my mom, told her what had happened, and asked if she had any books on spiritual warfare. She said she didn't, but would try to find something for me.

Later on, there was a knock on the door; it was Jerry. "Your mom says you guys are having some problems."

The place was a mess, but he didn't care. He went throughout the apartment and anointed each room with oil while praying. Afterwards, he recommended a series of tapes by Dean Sherman on the subject of spiritual warfare. He said I could borrow them from the church library.

All week I listened to the tapes while driving to the university and back. One thing that struck me is that Satan battles for the Christian's mind twenty-four hours a day, seven days a week. A Christian endures these attacks throughout his or her entire life. Satan will back off while we are spiritually strong, then hit us in our weakest area when we grow weary. A person like me doesn't have to worry about being tempted to steal money, because honesty has never been a problem. However, I would have to constantly be aware of sexual temptation. Each day I'd have to pray for strength in that area.

● ● ●

I was enjoying life as a born-again Christian, but my plans were still failing to materialize. During the fall semester of 1996, I felt going back into the Navy was an unrealistic idea, since my grades were not improving. Disappointed, I did not register for the second semester. Instead, I tested again for two police departments in California while returning to part time work in Hot Springs. Neither agency in California offered me a position, and the one I had in Montana was given to someone else. In March of 1997, I was an unemployed college dropout, but still at peace.

One Sunday after church I asked Jerry if we could get together. He came over to the apartment and said he could feel the difference inside. "It's not nearly as oppressive as the time before," he said.

After pouring us both a cup of coffee, I explained to him it had been over a year since the Plumb Line, and my Christian walk was great, but every door of opportunity was shut tight.

"It seems like I'm going to have to move out of this area in order to get a job, but I don't want to do anything the Lord doesn't approve of," I said.

"That's good, you should consult the Lord before making any big decisions, but you can't let fear stop you from doing what needs to be done. Sometimes the enemy will use fear as a way to keep us from carrying out God's will."

It made sense to me, but I still wasn't sure what I was to do or where to do it.

"If you could do any job, what would it be?" he asked.

While sipping my coffee, I thought hard. Playing cops and robbers no longer appealed to me. "I'm not sure. I guess I'd like to be a writer."

"Well, God can always use more writers. Pray about it."

When Jerry left, I surrendered the whole situation to God. "Okay Lord," I prayed, "I know what it is You don't want me to do, so please show me what it is You want me to do."

12
I WANT TO LIVE

*If we live, we live to the Lord; and if we die, we die to the Lord. So,
whether we live or die, we belong to the Lord.* Romans 14:8

FOUR MONTHS LATER I moved to Alameda, California and got
a job with a security company guarding the former Naval Air
Station. Going from a police officer to a security guard was
humbling, but I took it on faith God had something better in
mind for me. Felicia and the kids came out in October and we
moved into a small, expensive apartment and started attending
a local church.

I drove a small white pickup truck around the base from
10 P.M. to 6 A.M. When I got tired, I'd park on the tarmac,
pour myself a cup of coffee, and gaze at the lights of San Francisco and the Bay Bridge. I was shocked to hear radio talkers
mocking God in the name of tolerance, promoting perverted
lifestyles, and encouraging hatred towards Christians.

"Oh Lord, why do You allow that wicked city to mock You
and fester in sin? Why not destroy it?" I prayed.

My question was answered immediately. I sensed the Holy
Spirit saying to me, "Your prayer is like that of Jonah. Just
like the people of Nineveh, I do not wish for these people to
perish, but to repent. What if I had pronounced judgment on
the world when you were still in sin? Pray for the salvation of
the city, rather than its destruction."

My attitude changed. Instead of despising the people of San Francisco, I felt sorry for them. The gay community is enslaved to the power of Satan, so my prayers for them changed. The radio stations I listened to also changed. I found a couple of good Christian stations that provided solid teaching. At the end of my eight-hour shift I'd feel invigorated.

Over time, I also felt the Lord was telling me not to be ashamed of my past, because there are so many others who are trapped by sexual sin. If they knew my story, it would be possible for them to know there is hope.

The job at the base was enjoyable, but it could not meet our financial needs, and I felt the Lord was saying it was time to work someplace else. In December I was hired by Brinks Incorporated to work in their armored cars.

• • •

While working at the naval air station, I was able to be alone in my thoughts while listening to Christian radio. Things were different at Brinks. Along with the increase in pay came more responsibilities, deadlines, and interaction with my co-workers. My ATM run started about noon, and after delivering the deposits at the bank's cash vault in San Francisco, all of us would meet on Market Street for a break. The messengers and guards would visit while eating fast food meals. Usually the language was coarse, like it had been in the Navy, but now I was uncomfortable with it.

Rick Wisler had been the first person in my hiring group who had become a messenger, and now we were working together. As much as he tried to perfect the job, he just couldn't get the hang of it. Rick was twenty-two, but had already been married five years and had three children. He was about six feet and skinny with wavy blond hair. One night, after an especially difficult day, he confided in me that he was unhappy with the hand life had dealt him. This was not the first time he had done this, and usually I'd just listen to him in silence. On this occasion, I could feel the Holy Spirit prompting me to speak.

I was afraid to share my faith, but in obedience I opened my mouth and said, "Earlier today, you said something which indicated to me you believe in God. Am I right in assuming that?"

"Yeah, I believe in God. I used to go to Sunday school when I was a kid," he answered.

"It's possible He's trying to get your attention," I continued. "I know you've been through a lot, but God has saved others with problems just as bad or worse."

I told him my story, about how I'd been trapped in the snare of pornography and how I'd nearly killed myself, because those demons wouldn't let go of me. He was contemplating every word. Then I went on to tell him how Jesus saved me from the powers of hell.

"You were once suicidal?" Rick asked.

"Yeah."

"That's incredible. You've got everything together. I didn't think anything bad had ever happened to you."

He went on to admit that he'd struggled with pornography as long as he could remember and was sexually active in his teen years. The only reason he'd married his wife was because he'd gotten her pregnant in high school. They'd dropped out, and she cared for the baby while he worked at one job after another. From the sounds of it, there wasn't much love in the marriage. Each of them had been unfaithful to the other at least once.

"I don't have any magic solutions, but if you commit your life to Christ you'll be off to a good start," I said. "You also need to join a Bible-believing church, spend time in the Word, and get as much Christian teaching as you can from TV or radio."

"I've really tried not to go into adult bookstores and not to lust for other women, but I can't help it," he said in desperation.

"Then you may have to do what I did, and that's confess your sin to other Christians," I answered.

"Why is that necessary?" he asked.

"Because pride is a powerful sin, and any sin in your life will keep you from receiving the blessings God has for you. When you confess those sins, it's humiliating and that's what kills pride. You don't have to go before a group like I did, but you should at least make your confession to a pastor or church elder. Afterwards, he can pray for you and give you counsel. I'm not saying this is the only way to break free from your sin, but confession is what worked for me."

Over the next couple of weeks Rick and his wife joined a Baptist Church and made an appointment to meet with the pastor privately. Every day after that conversation, he'd have a series of questions for me. I answered them as best I could and would sometimes look up scripture for him. Rick eventually left the company and completed the police academy in Eureka, California. He called me one night to tell me his brother had accepted Christ while watching The 700 Club, and he was now counseling him.

· · ·

In mid-November 2002, I was sitting in the back of Brinks truck 982124 with my guard Dana Jackson while drinking coffee in the town of Hercules. The gray truck with blue trim was becoming a regular sight in the small shopping center's parking lot. Dana was from an inner city neighborhood in Oakland and had worked with me at the Naval Air Station. When she heard I was going to Brinks she wanted to come with me.

We always took our break in that parking lot before finishing our last two stops. I'd discovered the coffee shop while attending a Christian writer's conference in Hercules the year before. That afternoon, Dana told me about a friend of hers who was running an escort service in San Francisco. The woman she was talking about had been terminated from Brinks, but they had remained close friends.

"So what do you think?" Dana asked me.

"I think it's a dangerous job, and she should find something else to do."

"It's not that dangerous; she doesn't actually have sex with the men. She just supervises the girls who do. She'll only go out with the men if they're really shorthanded."

Once again, I felt the Lord prompting me to speak. "Let me tell you something. I know a little more about that type of work than you may think."

"You?" Dana said surprised.

I told her my story. She became teary eyed and told me things about her own past. Dana was a single parent with a six-year-old son, and she was hoping that someday she would meet a decent man to marry.

"I've been going to the same church, off and on, since I was a kid, but it's hard to live a godly life in my neighborhood," she said.

"Believe me, I know being a Christian isn't easy," I assured her. "You said the pastor keeps wanting to talk to you, so get with him and let him help."

"Okay Jake, I will," she said cheerfully, wiping her eyes with a tissue.

A week later, on Thursday the 21st, the truck made its way to our last stop in Berkeley. It'd been a tiring day. The driver was the fourth one I'd had that week. It was his first time driving solo and he was so afraid of making mistakes, he kept making them. If I said left he went right, if I said reverse he went forward. That's how it went all day. Finally, he parked the truck on Potter Street in front of the small Wells Fargo Bank that served as a local business center.

While exiting the truck, with my coal bag and a night drop

bag, which were both empty, Dana talked about her family. Other than a confused driver, it had been a typical workday, the weather was sunny and pleasant and I hardly noticed the white SUV backed up to the bank lobby on our right. Windows at the south end (street side) and east end (parking lot side) of the lobby made the inside feel like a greenhouse, so the front door had been propped open for air. Inside the lobby, I could clearly see the truck through the open door and the surrounding windows.

While entering the code into the alarm keypad above the ATM, I listened to the customers and tellers in the bank to my right. Dana stood by the open door on my left, still talking. The girl talked so much, I'd have to tune her out so I could concentrate on the alarm code. I didn't mind her talking, though, since it helped the day go faster. Everything was routine until Dana stopped in mid-sentence.

"Watch out!" she said in an ominous tone. Running foot-steps could be heard outside.

Fear gripped me as I turned in her direction. There was a medium sized black man standing in the doorway only inches from Dana. He was dressed in black sweats, white running shoes, and white gloves. Through the slit of his black ski mask, wide brown eyes looked at Dana, then at me. In his hands he held an AK-47 assault rifle with a banana clip.

Several things happened in a matter of seconds and a million thoughts ran through my mind. I could surrender, but since I didn't have money on me I would've been forced to open the safes at gunpoint. For all I knew, they would kill us anyway. Giving up to some punks violated all the criminal justice training I'd gone through over the years. Although out-gunned, I pulled my revolver from its holster and decided to fight.

The gunman in the doorway was quickly trying to aim his rifle at me while I attempted to align the sights of my .38

special on him. At the firing range, we're given several seconds to pick our target, but in reality there isn't time for aiming. I started shooting, but was only able to get off two rounds. The window by the door shattered. There was another gunman standing in the parking lot who fired from a carbine.

The window to my left exploded, and I felt as if a three-hundred pound defensive lineman had hit me. I was knocked off my feet and suddenly was looking up at the ceiling. My body went into shock and the .38 slipped out of my hands. Now for the first time in my life I thought I was going to die, and I didn't want to. After all those numerous thoughts of suicide I couldn't believe it was actually going to happen.

Is this how it ends, Lord? I prayed. *I don't want to die yet, there's still too much to live for. Please Jesus, I want to live.*

The first draft of this book was finished, query letters had been sent to Christian publishers across the country, and I refused to believe this is how it was to end. My life didn't flash before my eyes, but I could see the faces of my children pleading with me not to go. I could no longer fight, though, and I felt like a wounded deer waiting for the hunter to finish him off.

A loud burst of automatic gunfire came from the AK-47, hitting Dana twice in the back and blowing out most of the plaster around the ATM. Our driver drove off with the truck and called for help. The gunman in the doorway ran over to me, grabbed the empty bags, and jumped through the broken window to the waiting SUV. The getaway vehicle sped out of the parking lot and turned onto Ashby Avenue. Just as quickly as it began, the attack ended. I was covered with glass and plaster and there was a smell of cordite in the air. A crimson circle was expanding on the right side of my shirt.

Dana lay in the doorway. Her breathing was loud, raspy, and rapid. The sound was terrible, and I could tell she'd been shot through the lungs. Then her breathing stopped. After a couple of seconds, the people in the bank came over to check on us.

A customer knelt beside me and asked, "What's your name?"

"Jake."

"Jake, I'm Carrie. Hang in there, help is on the way."

Carla, the bank manager, ran into the lobby and said, "Oh my God, no, this can't be happening." She was a thin black woman with gray braids who immediately took charge of the scene. "Erica, call 9-1-1, Brinks has been shot!"

I've met some pretty calloused characters in my day, but this one customer took the prize. This man from outside was filling out a deposit slip and tried stepping over Dana's body. "Sir, get out! We're closed for business," shouted Carla.

Erica, the teller, came over to check on me. Only recently had we discovered we attended the same church. She was still in her twenties, with dark skin and long brown curly hair. She said my name, but that was all. The carnage was too much for her; she hurried back into the bank.

A fireman came and looked at Dana then came over to me. When a second came in, the first said, "Leave her alone and give me a hand with this guy."

The two paramedics snipped away the laces on my boots and cut away my uniform.

A police officer secured my gun, then walked over to the doorway. Looking down at Dana, he spoke into the shoulder microphone of his radio. "Dispatch, you better send out homicide."

When the firemen and ambulance crew loaded me onto the gurney they had to lift me over the corpse. They loaded me into the ambulance, which took me to a hospital in Oakland.

At first, nothing made sense. Why would God rescue me from one tribulation, just to throw me into another? A single .223 round had grazed the back of my right thigh, ricocheted off the ATM wall, entered my right side below the rib cage, and exploded. The surgeons removed two fragments near my spine, but left the others for fear of doing more damage.

I lay in that hospital bed for a week re-living the incident in my mind. My fears were alleviated by the overwhelming love and concern from so many people. Most of my hospital stay was spent on the phone with co-workers, relatives, friends, and Wells Fargo employees. A security guard at the hospital, who I didn't know, gave me a note of encouragement, and our church made sure there were hot meals at the apartment. I felt like George Bailey at the end of *It's A Wonderful Life*. Memories of my past came to mind, and I comprehended how selfish and devastating suicide is. And I realized that there are guardian angels. That bullet fragmented into about twenty pieces, but not one of my internal organs was damaged and no bones were broken.

The love between Felicia and I grew stronger that week than at any other time in our marriage. Her employer was kind enough to give her the necessary time off, and she spent every night at my side. I kept thanking her for being there and for her obstinate devotion to me. She helped me in and out of bed, bathed me, and emptied my white plastic bottle when it was full. It still perplexed me how God could bless me with such a faithful wife after all my terrible sins. The love God has for us cannot be grasped by the human mind.

During the day, my mom and the kids stayed with me so Felicia could go home for a shower and nap. Mom was having a terrible month. Two weeks earlier, Dad was almost killed while hunting with a friend. The camper they were sleeping in exploded from a leaking propane tank. He suffered third- and second-degree burns, and my mom was still caring for him when Felicia called, and she came. On Thanksgiving Day I was released. Mom prepared the dinner. But I had no appetite.

When I returned to work in February, my co-workers

continued to show their support for me. There were numerous handshakes and hugs. I returned to my old route as a guard, and received the same treatment at the banks. At the small Wells Fargo business center in Berkeley, I stood on the spot where I had lain bleeding. The spot where Dana had died and where the first gunman had stood was seven feet away. Briefly, I was alone with my thoughts. *How could I have missed? If I had hit him maybe Dana would have lived. What was this all about, Lord?*

I still don't have a definite answer, but my eyes have been opened to how God has blessed me with a great wife, children, parents, and friends. Everything is in God's hands. I believe He decides when it is time for us to die and not anything or anybody can alter that. Since He allowed me to live, it has reaffirmed my commitment to share my story with others. God can take us from this world at any moment.

And I'm at peace with that.

EPILOGUE

A perverse heart shall depart from me; I will know no evil.
Psalm 101:4 (NASB)

THIEVERY AND DRUG USE have always been easy for me to resist, so the devil tempts me with lust, because he knows that is my weakness. After being forgiven from all those terrible sins, there is still a constant battle for my mind. I have to always be careful not to become the proverbial dog who returns to its vomit or like the Israelites who thought eating fresh vegetables in slavery was better than eating manna while free. The difference now is I no longer *have* to lust. My flesh may still *want* to, but my spirit's desire to please God is stronger.

If you're thinking, "Hey, I want to please God, too. But sometimes the temptation is so great I give in" . . . remember, just because we are now Christians does not mean we stop being human. In modern America we're bombarded with sexual images and our thoughts may cause us to sin. But if we do, that doesn't mean we lose our salvation.

In John 13, Jesus washes the feet of His disciples. Peter protested and said, "No, You shall never wash my feet."

Jesus said, "Unless I wash you, you have no part with me."

"Then Lord, not just my feet but my hands and my head as well," replied Peter.

Jesus answered, "He who has bathed needs only to wash his feet, but is completely clean; and you are clean . . ."

Jesus isn't just speaking to Peter; He's speaking to you and me. He knows we walk through this sinful world and our feet are going to get dirty. When you sin, approach Christ with a contrite heart and confess what you've done. You don't need to ask for salvation or set up a meeting with your wife and pastor.

So why does God allow the devil to constantly attack me in this weak area of my life? The answer is found in Second Corinthians 12. Paul had a weakness, which he called a thorn in his flesh. A demon was buffeting Paul, and he asked God three times that it might depart from him.

> But He said to me, 'My grace is sufficient for you, for My power is made perfect in weakness.' Therefore I will boast all the more gladly about my weaknesses, so that Christ's power may rest on me. (II Corinthians 12:9)

In applying those words to my own life I can conclude that my weakness against lust is my strength against pride.

> But He gives us more grace. That is why Scripture says: 'God opposes the proud but gives grace to the humble.' (James 4:6)

God's grace does not give us a license to sin; it frees us from the bondage to sin. If Jesus was physically present, no Christian would spit in His face, but that is what we're doing when we choose to deliberately sin. During my research of spiritual warfare, I discovered that we either serve God or Satan, because there is no neutral territory. Anything you put in place of God is idolatry. The sex addict may not always make time for daily devotions, but he will look at pornography at each opportunity and will usually end up masturbating sometime during the day. It isn't something he wants to do, but it's something he has to do.

When you read the Old Testament, you probably wonder why so many of the kings of Israel and Judah would turn to those imbecilic idols. When they followed God's commandments He allowed them to prosper, but when they worshiped Baal, foreign invaders occupied their cities. What made those figurines of stone and bronze so appealing? It was the demon behind them.

II Chronicles 25:2 says King Amaziah "did right in the sight of the Lord, yet not with a whole heart."

Is that you? Do you walk in the Lord's ways, yet occasionally succumb to the Baal of pornography—perhaps out of "curiosity?"

Addictions are something we use to medicate ourselves from the pains we experience in life. Those pains can stem from failure, loss of a loved one, financial ruin, or any number of things. Something happened to the addict, so he turned to pornography, which led to sexual behavior he wants to keep secret. In my case, I experienced rejection, and instead of seeking God's will for my life, I rebelled. I knew sex outside of marriage was wrong, but that was what I chose to ease my pain. In I Samuel 15:23 (KJV) the prophet Samuel tells King Saul, "For rebellion is as the sin of witchcraft, and stubbornness is as iniquity and idolatry."

I viewed pornographic material and fornicated, which made me guilty of idol worship and witchcraft. During no part of my life had I ever made a conscious effort to worship an idol or cast a spell. Taking part in anything of the occult had always scared me because of its blatant ties to Satanism. That's how Satan works; he blinds us and slowly, gradually leads us away from the truth. Perhaps you think that when you attend church and give your offerings, it will somehow offset those late night hours viewing cyberporn. It's maddening, because you can't figure out why you're feeling depressed or suicidal or why everything you do ends in failure. Paul writes:

> Do I mean then that a sacrifice offered to an idol is
> anything, or that an idol is anything? No, but the sacrifices
> of pagans are offered to demons, not to God, and I do
> not want you to be participants with demons. You cannot
> drink the cup of the Lord and the cup of demons too; you
> cannot have a part in both the Lord's table and the table
> of demons. (I Corinthians 10:19-21)

Paul was writing to church members who came from the pagan background of the Greeks. Within the city of Corinth there were thousands of temple prostitutes representing the goddess Aphrodite. Her very name is the root word for aphrodisiakos or aphrodisiac, meaning to arouse or increase sexual desire. It would have been very difficult for a new Christian to disengage from the lifestyle of that city and follow his new faith. Many of the church members still participated in acts of immorality, because the demonic nature still held them in bondage. The city was so well known for its decadence that the Greek verb Korinthiazoma, which means to fornicate, was derived from its name.

In his first letter to the church in Corinth, Paul warns that those who practice immorality shall not enter heaven.

> Do you not know that the wicked will not inherit the
> kingdom of God? Do not be deceived: Neither the sexu-
> ally immoral nor idolaters nor adulterers nor male prosti-
> tutes nor homosexual offenders nor thieves nor the greedy
> nor drunkards nor slanderers nor swindlers will inherit the
> kingdom of God. (I Corinthians 6:9,10)

In this passage, Paul clearly shows the links between idolatry and sexual immorality. The Christians of Corinth were suffering from that with which many Christians in America today are struggling—an epidemic of sexual stimuli and temptations.

It has been said that marijuana is the gateway to narcotics.

In the same sense, porn is the gateway to sex addiction. I started by looking at *Playboy* and *Penthouse* magazines with a kid who lived across the street. When we grew tired of those, he stole others from a liquor store. Even the stolen issues became boring when we found a copy of *Hustler* in a vacant lot. After I started watching X-rated videos, looking at an issue of *Playboy* was like a heroin junkie smoking a joint.

•   •   •

Perhaps you're asking, "What should I do if I'm the wife of a sex addict?" In that case, I recommend *An Affair of the Mind* by Laurie Hall. This book delves into the spiritual nature of sexuality while using Laurie's own story as a backdrop. For several years her husband was viewing pornography, visiting strip clubs, and picking up prostitutes. Eventually, he gave her an STD. She prayed for her husband for over twenty years until he was able to break free. If your husband is addicted to porn, you know how devastating it is to the family. Don't blame yourself, because it isn't your fault.

Laurie gives lots of advice for wives, but warns that there's no guarantee of a happy ending. Her plan is outlined from the Kenny Rogers song "The Gambler," as follows:

Know When to Hold 'Em.

If you've tried talking to him about his problem and there is no response, then stop trying. Don't ask him why he keeps looking at trashy magazines and don't remind him of his broken promises. By not talking, you can observe his behavior patterns. Talk also gives him an avenue for manipulation and he'll make the same empty promises like always. As you've probably learned, talking doesn't work. You need to admit your husband is not obeying the Word of God. I Peter 3:1 says unbelieving men will be won over, not by conversation, but by the actions of their wives.

Know When to Fold 'Em.

You reach the point where you say, "This isn't working." No matter what you do or say, your life is filled with shame and judgment. Pray that God will show your husband the evil in his life. Laurie says her husband's addiction dried up all their money and maxed out their credit cards. You might have to pay your bills, get a separate checking account, file a separate tax return, or get your own credit cards.

Know When to Walk Away.

His shame may boil over to anger, and he becomes verbally and physically abusive to you and the children. No matter how charming you act around him he explodes at the slightest provocation. Proverbs 22:24 says, "Do not make friends with a hot tempered man, do not associate with one easily angered." Make arrangements to stay with a friend or relative who will take you in at a moment's notice. Have an overnight bag packed and ready to go. When he becomes violent, take the kids and get out. Sometimes this is enough to force him into seeking help.

Know When to Run.

Don't run when you can walk. However, if your husband is sexually abusing the children, get out permanently and call the police. Laurie calls this a Lose-Win situation. Consider your husband gone, so now you need to try and salvage your children's welfare.

Clearly, pornography is not some harmless vice.

• • •

Maybe after reading my testimony, you are thinking that you have never fornicated or committed adultery. The Pharisees thought of themselves as being sexually pure, but Jesus knew they had lust in their hearts. He said,

> You have heard that it was said, 'Do not commit adultery.'
> But I tell you that anyone who looks at a woman lustfully
> has already committed adultery with her in his heart.
> (Matthew 5: 27-28)

In the next few verses, Jesus says if your eye causes you to lust then gouge it out. It is better to enter heaven minus an eye than to have your whole body cast into hell. Jesus calls us to purity by any means necessary. Burn those pornographic magazines and videotapes; there is no reason for them to be in the Christian home. There may be other magazines, books, catalogs, newspapers, or calendars that you need to throw away. If you are honest with yourself, it is easy to identify those things that act as a triggering device and cause impure thoughts.

Use some self discipline to keep inappropriate thoughts and actions in check. Paul writes:

> It is God's will that you should be sanctified; that you
> should avoid sexual immorality; that each of you should
> learn to control his own body in a way that is holy and
> honorable, not in passionate lust like the heathen, who
> do not know God; and that in this matter no one should
> wrong his brother or take advantage of him. The Lord
> will punish men for all such sins, as we have already
> told you and warned you. For God did not call us to be
> impure, but to live a holy life. Therefore, he who rejects
> this instruction does not reject man but God, who gives
> you His Holy Spirit. (I Thessalonians 4:3-8)

When we're free from those addictive sins we can fulfill the plans God has for us and experience His abundant blessings.

Right now you may be asking, "That may have worked for you, but what about me? I've never heard of a Plumb Line so how can I attend one? I've tried everything I can think of and nothing seems to work. Where can I turn for help?"

In *The War Within: Gaining Victory in the Battle for Sexual*

Purity Robert Daniels says we should develop a Purity Plan. You're praying or reading the Bible when lustful thoughts hit you. It's a demonic attack, and you can quote James 4:7:

> Submit yourself, then, to God. Resist the devil, and he will flee from you. Come near to God and he will come near to you.

And remember II Corinthians 10:5:

> We demolish arguments and every pretension that sets itself up against the knowledge of God, and we take captive every thought to make it obedient to Christ.

Resist by stating aloud, "I resist the devil in the name and through the blood of Jesus Christ, my savior." Meditate on Romans 6:1-4. Reckon yourself dead to sin, and keep in mind: those flaming darts can lead to sinful thoughts and actions.

We are constantly being assailed by sexual images from the world. Movies and television shows can act as trigger devices. If a TV show is tripping you up then turn the channel. Don't watch movies you wouldn't want your kids or grandmother to see you viewing. If an acquaintance is telling a dirty joke or talking about his sexual exploits, change the subject or walk away. This has worked for me.

Daniels also says if we know ahead of time of potential exposure, to form a plan. Perhaps your job requires you to travel and you'll be staying in hotels that show X-rated movies. Friends or clients might want to take you to a strip club. Maybe your wife will be out of town and you'll be home alone. Fast and pray and have others pray for you. If necessary, have the hotel remove the TV from your room. You might have to remove the TV and VCR from your home. Call home every night and set objectives for your free time. When you return from a trip, set up an accountability session with your wife or with a trusted friend. Have them ask those tough questions.

By maturing as Christians our resistance to the devil will strengthen. Romans 8:29 tells us to focus on spiritual growth. Since the sinful nature will not allow us to dwell on godly thoughts, the Holy Spirit must dwell within us.

> The mind of sinful man is death, but the mind controlled by the Spirit is life and peace; the sinful mind is hostile to God. It does not submit to God's law, nor can it do so. Those controlled by the sinful nature cannot please God. You, however, are controlled not by the sinful nature but by the Spirit, if the Spirit of God lives in you. And if anyone does not have the Spirit of Christ, he does not belong to Christ. (Romans 8:6-9)

Galatians 5 says if we live in the Holy Spirit we will not be doing what our sinful nature craves. If we belong to Christ, we have nailed our sinful desires and passions to the Cross. When the Holy Spirit controls our lives He will produce love, joy, peace, patience, kindness, goodness, faithfulness, gentleness, and self control.

If you're attending a Bible-believing church, God has provided a pastor and a body of elders to assist in your Christian walk. In Chapter Eleven of this book I shared how confessing to a group of fellow Christians broke the chains of bondage. The church elders can listen to your own confession and pray for you afterwards.

> It was He who gave some to be apostles, some to be prophets, some to be evangelists, and some to be pastors and teachers, to prepare God's people for works of service, so that the body of Christ may be built up until we all reach unity in the faith and in the knowledge of the Son of God and become mature, attaining to the whole measure of the fullness of Christ. (Ephesians 4:11-13)

Associate with other committed Christians. Attend church regularly, participate in a home fellowship, attend Promise Keepers. You may consider joining a men's group that specializes in sex addiction. "And let us consider how we may spur one another on toward love and good deeds." (Heb. 10:24)

We have to discipline ourselves to set aside regular times for praying, reading the Bible, meditating on and memorizing scripture, and worship. When first arriving at boot camp, I thought there was no way I could make it through. My drill instructors demanded perfection, even when it came to lacing my shoes. After a couple of weeks it became routine and I left that place aware of the lazy and slothful habits I came in with.

Disciplining ourselves can be rough, but it's essential we do this; that's why we are called disciples. God doesn't want lazy Christians. I get up an hour early every morning before work for my daily devotions. For me, it means getting up at 4 or 5 A.M. We should give Him a hundred percent production when disciplining ourselves. If you clean the restrooms at your church, remember you're doing it for His glory. Devote yourself fully to God, continue to seek help, remember the Lord's grace, and you'll be able to keep your addiction under control.

Appendix

Sexual Addiction Internet Websites

http://sexaa.org
http://avenueresource.com
http://youthapostles.com
http://christiananswers.net
http://christians-in-recovery.org
http://goodmorals.org
http://prodigalsonline.org
http://sexaddict.com
http://sa.org

See also:
http://www.ransomedheart.com

Glossary of Naval Terms and Acronyms

1MC – The ship-wide public address system

3M – Maintenance and Material Management

AA – Airman Apprentice (pay grade E-2 in the aviation field)

AIM – Air-Intercept-Missile

AN – Airman (pay grade E-3)

AO – Aviation Ordnanceman

AR – Airman Recruit, the lowest rank in the Navy (pay grade E-1)

AWSEP – Aviation Weapons Support Equipment Program

BDU – Battle Dress Uniform

Blue Nose – A sailor who crossed the Arctic (or Antarctic) Circle

BM – Boatswain Mate

Bulkhead – A ship's wall

Captain's Mast – Non-judicial punishment for enlisted personnel (Article 15 of the UCMJ)

CC – Company Commander (a Navy drill instructor)

Chow – Food

Cinderella Liberty – Get back to the ship by midnight

CO – Commanding Officer (a ship's captain)

COD – Carrier Onboard Delivery by the C-2 aircraft (also called Miss Piggy)

Corpsman – A sailor who serves as a medic for the Navy and Marine Corps

CPO – Chief Petty Officer (Pay grade E-7)

CWO – Chief Warrant Officer

DC – Damage Control

DCPO – Damage Control Petty Officer

Deck – Floors on a ship

E-Club – Enlisted men's Club

EMI – Extra Military Instruction (Usually additional work assigned as punishment during liberty hours)

Ensign – The American flag, flown from the stern while anchored and from the main mast while at sea (also the lowest rank for commissioned officers)

EOD – Explosive Ordnance Disposal

FA – Fireman Apprentice (an E-2 in the engineering field)

Gedunk – Snack food (Used as a meal substitute when chow was exceptionally bad)

GM – Gunner's Mate

Gun Boss – Commanding officer for a ship's weapons department

Gun Deck – Signing off maintenance that was not performed

Gunner – A warrant officer in charge of a weapons division

Hawkeye – E-2C Early warning aircraft

Head, The – Toilet and shower room on Navy installations

Helo – Helicopter

Hornet – F/A-18 (a duel purpose aircraft that can attack ground targets and fight enemy aircraft)

IO, The – The Indian Ocean

Khakis – A slang term in reference to chiefs and officers, because of their working uniforms

Leave – Vacation

LGB – Laser Guided Bomb (smart bomb)

Liberty – Off duty hours while in port

LPO – Leading Petty Officer

MAA – Master-At-Arms (a ship's security force)

Med, The – The Mediterranean Sea

MEPS – Military Enlistment Processing Station

MM – Machinist's Mate

MS – Mess Specialist (A Navy cook)

NAS – Naval Air Station

OC – Ordnance Control

OOD – Officer of the Deck

Overhead – A ceiling within a ship

Petty Officer – Mid-level ranks for enlisted personnel (pay grades E-4 through E-6)

PH – Photographer's Mate

PN – Personnelman

Pollywog – A sailor who has not crossed the equator

PT – Physical Training

Rack – A bed

R&O – Receiving and Outfitting

Rate – A sailor's job specialty

Rockeye – A cluster bomb

RTC – Recruit Training Command

SAR – Search and Rescue

Scuttlebutt – Rumor, gossip

Shell Back – A sailor who has crossed the equator

Skid Stow – Storage area for ordnance handling equipment

Sortie – A specific mission carried out by an aircraft

Spot Check – An inspection of preventive maintenance

TAD – Temporary Assigned Duty

UA – Unauthorized Absence

UCMJ – Uniform Code of Military Justice

Union Jack – A replica of the blue, star-studded field of the American flag that is flown from a ship's bow while moored or anchored

XO – Executive Officer (Officer who is second in command of a ship)

SOURCES

Daniels, Robert. *The War Within: Gaining Victory in the Battle for Sexual Purity.* (Wheaton, IL: Crossway Books, 1997)

Hall, Laurie. *An Affair of the Mind: One Woman's Courageous Battle to Salvage Her Family From the Devastation of Pornography.* (Wheaton, IL: Tyndale House Publishers, 1996)

Hayford, Pastor Jack. *Why Sex Sins are Worse than Others.* (Cassette C0179. Living Way Ministries)

Prince, Derek. *Blessing or Curse: You Can Choose.* (Grand Rapids, MI: Chosen Books, 1990)

About the Author

Jake Porter is a pen name used by the author, John Buzzard. He resides in Arizona with his wife, Eva, and their German shepherd, Rocky.

For his service in the United States Navy, John received the following citations: Navy Unit Commendation, Good Conduct Medal, National Defense Medal, Armed Forces Expedition Medal, South-West Asia Service Medal (with 3 stars), Sea Service Ribbon (with 2 stars), Liberation of Kuwait Medal (Saudi Arabia), and Liberation of Kuwait Medal (Kuwait).

He later served as a civilian mariner with the Navy's Military Sealift Command.

John enjoys learning and writing about the Old West. His first historical novel, *That Day by the Creek: A Novel About the Sand Creek Massacre of 1864*, was released by Cladach in 2016.

To learn more, find John online:
https://www.facebook.com/JohnBuzzardWriter/
https://cladach.com/authors/john-buzzard/

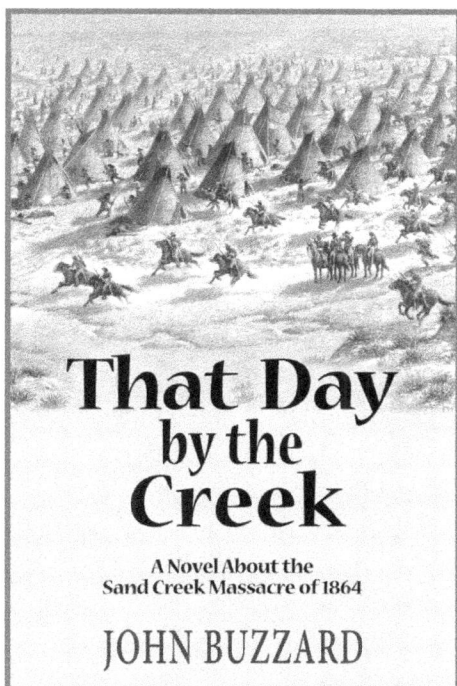